Color Test Page

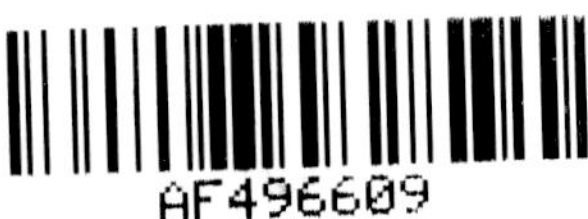

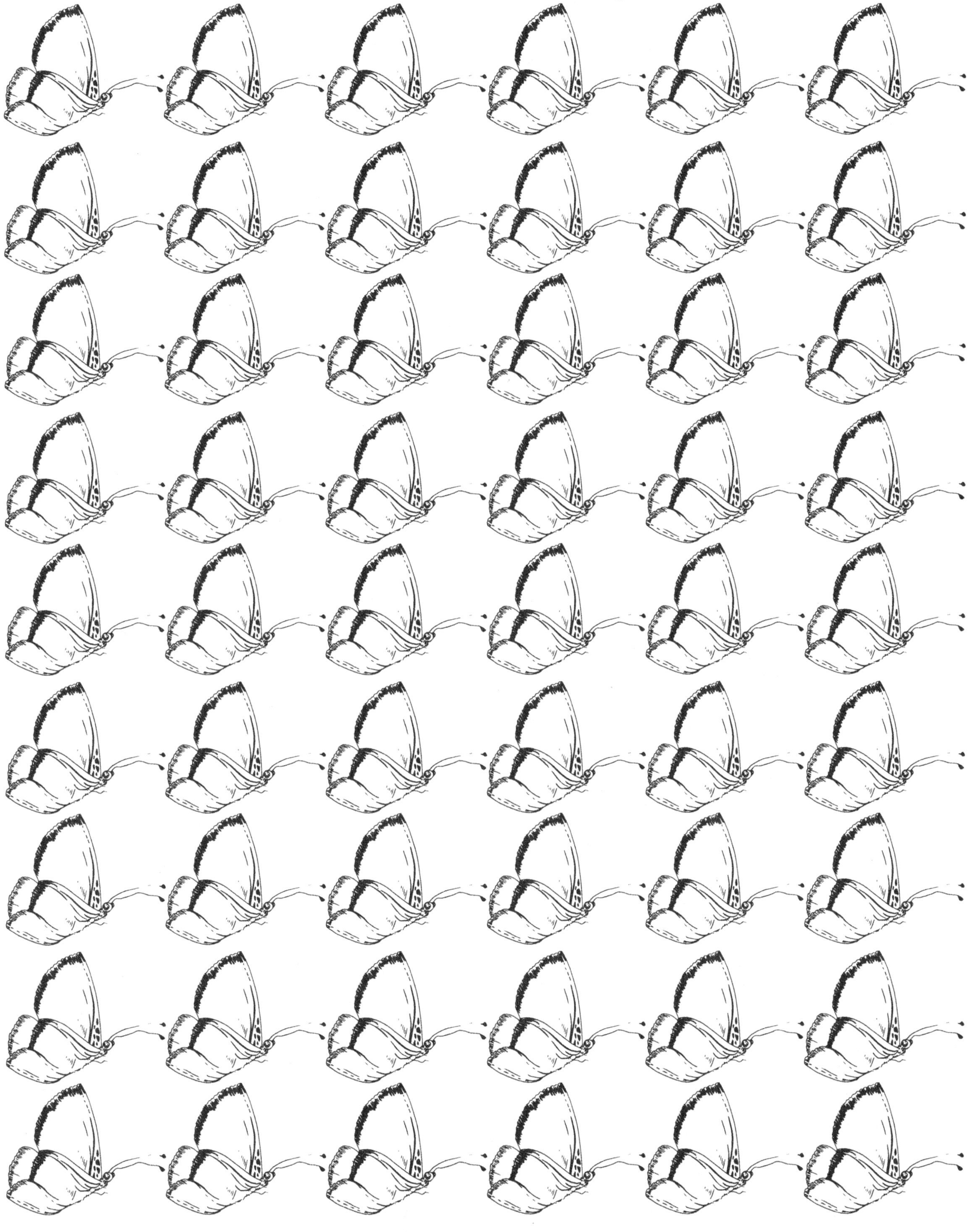

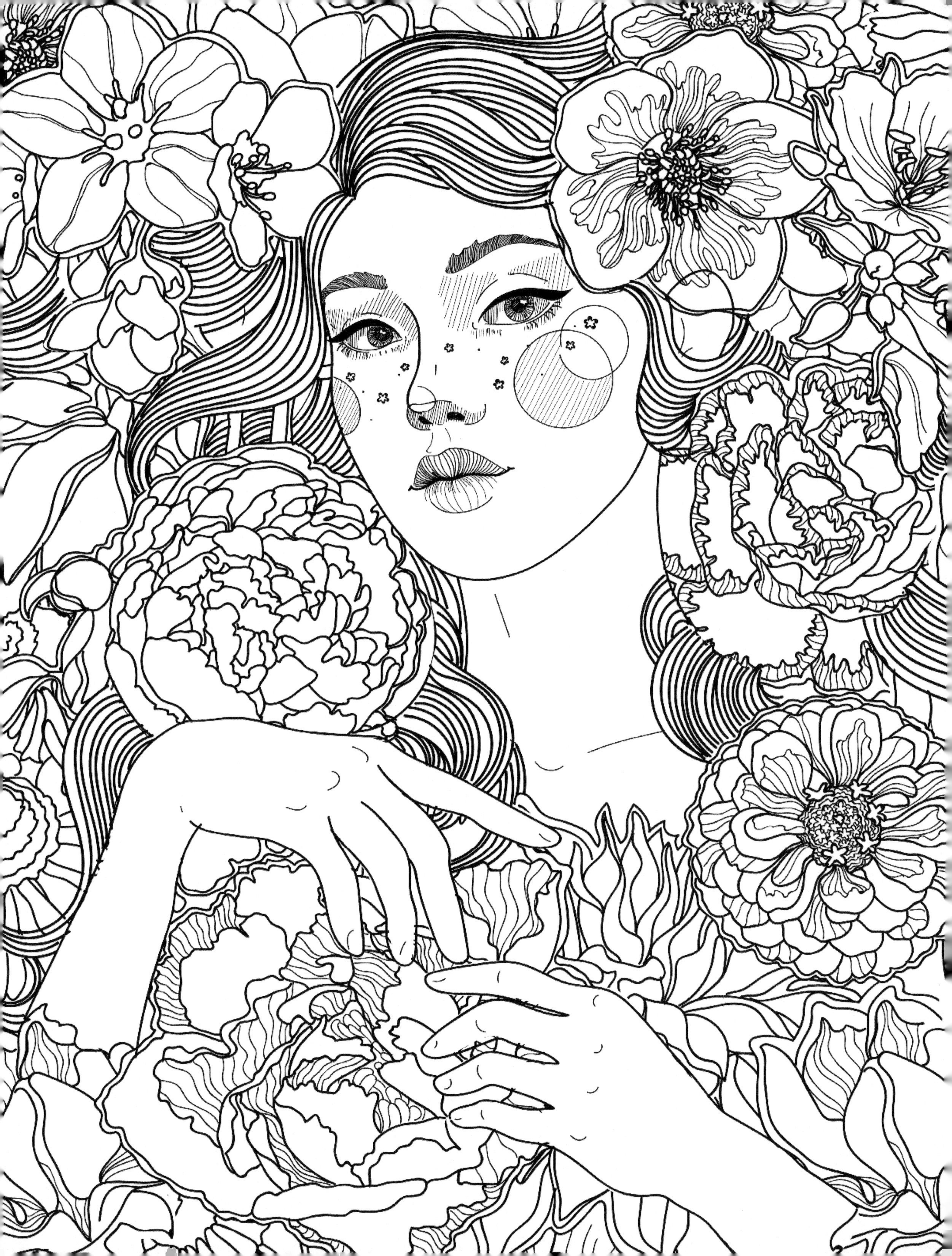

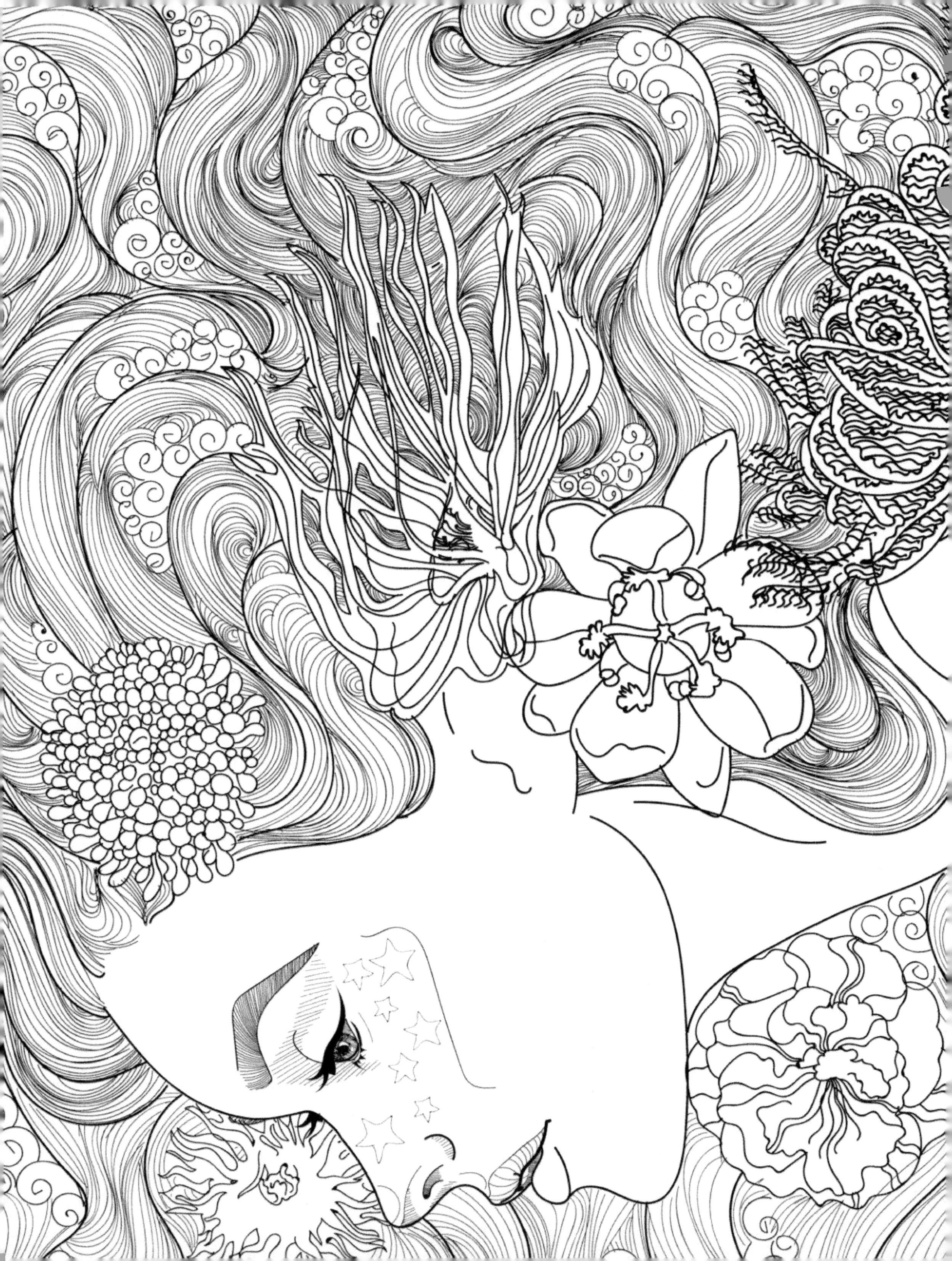

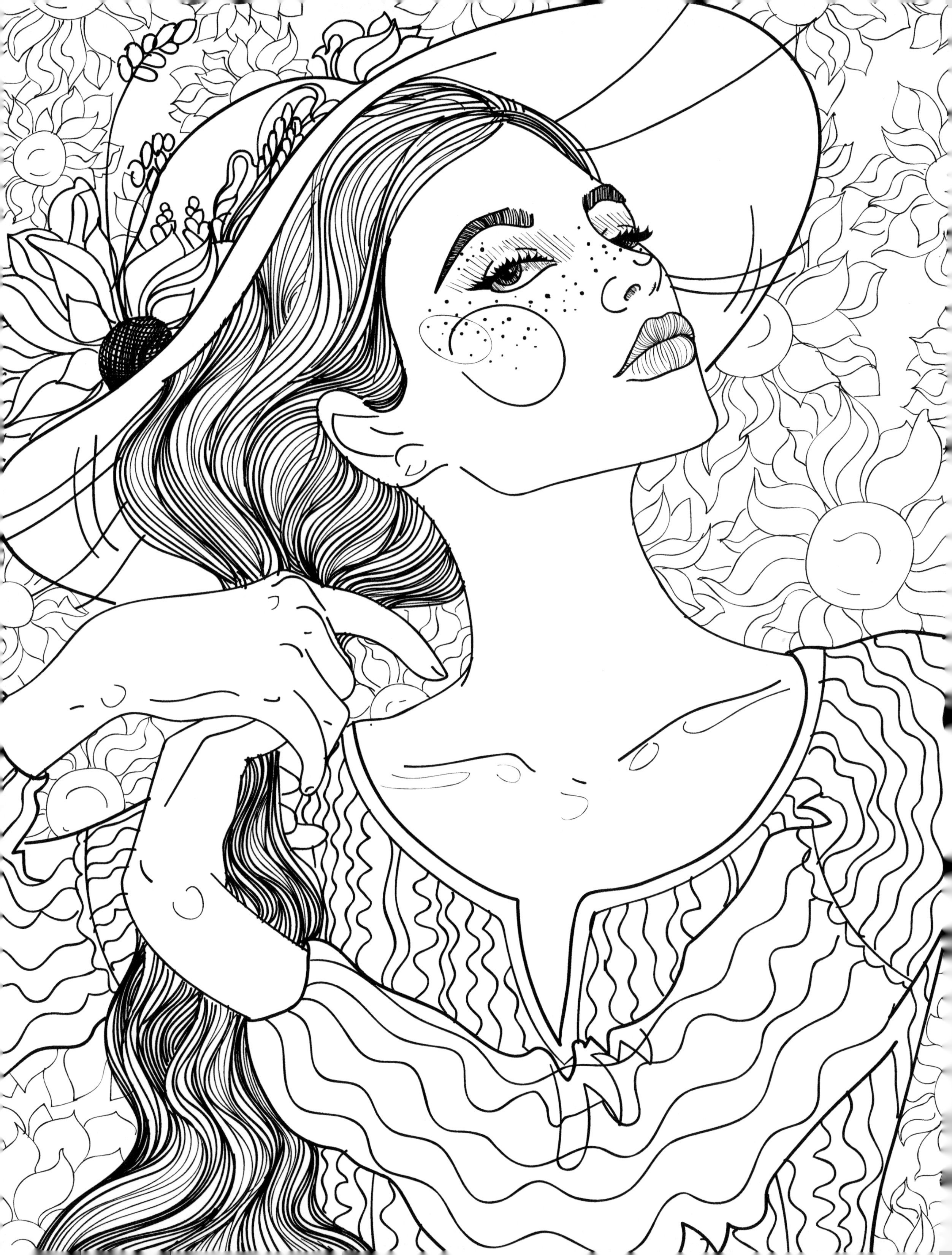

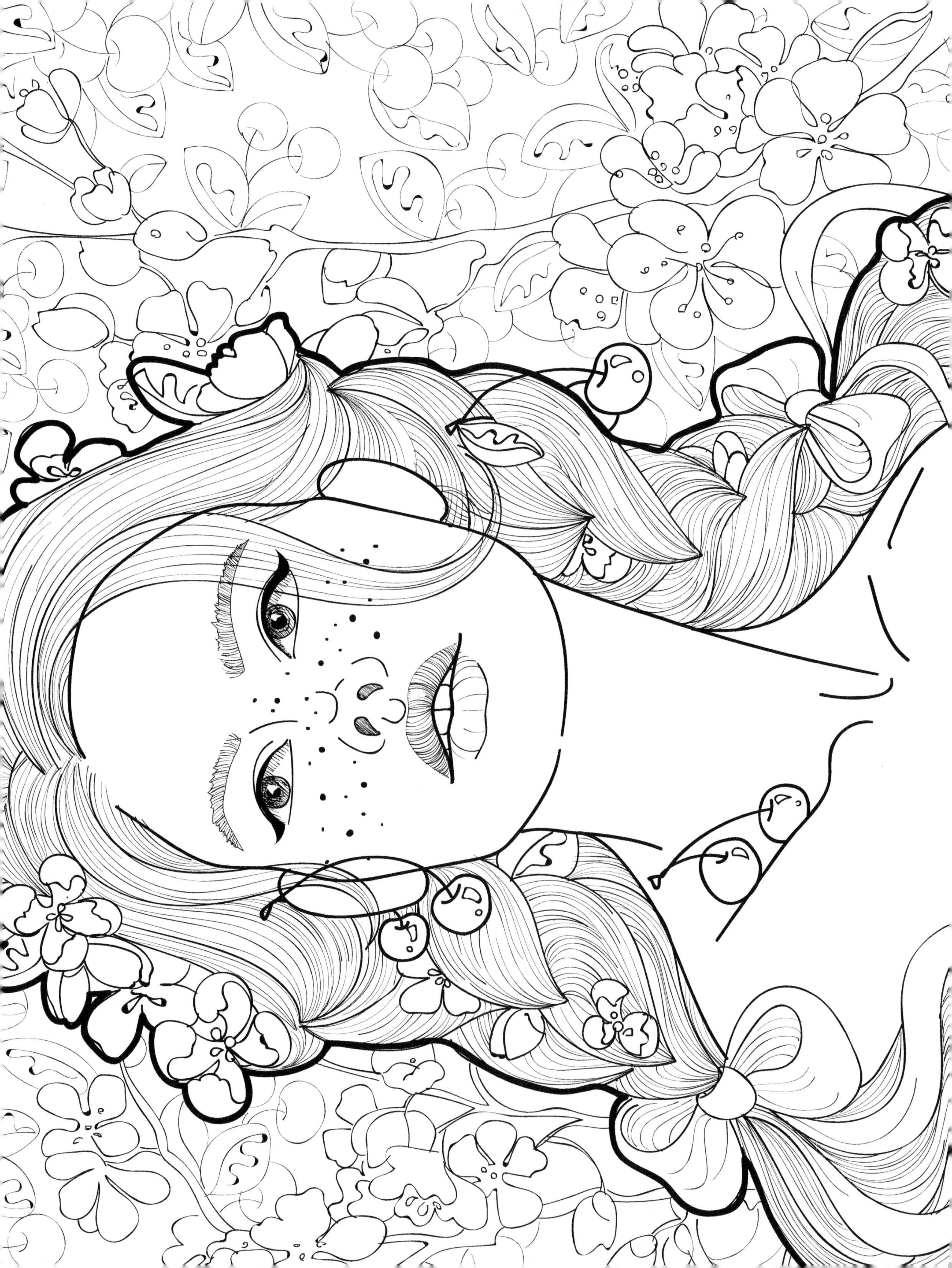

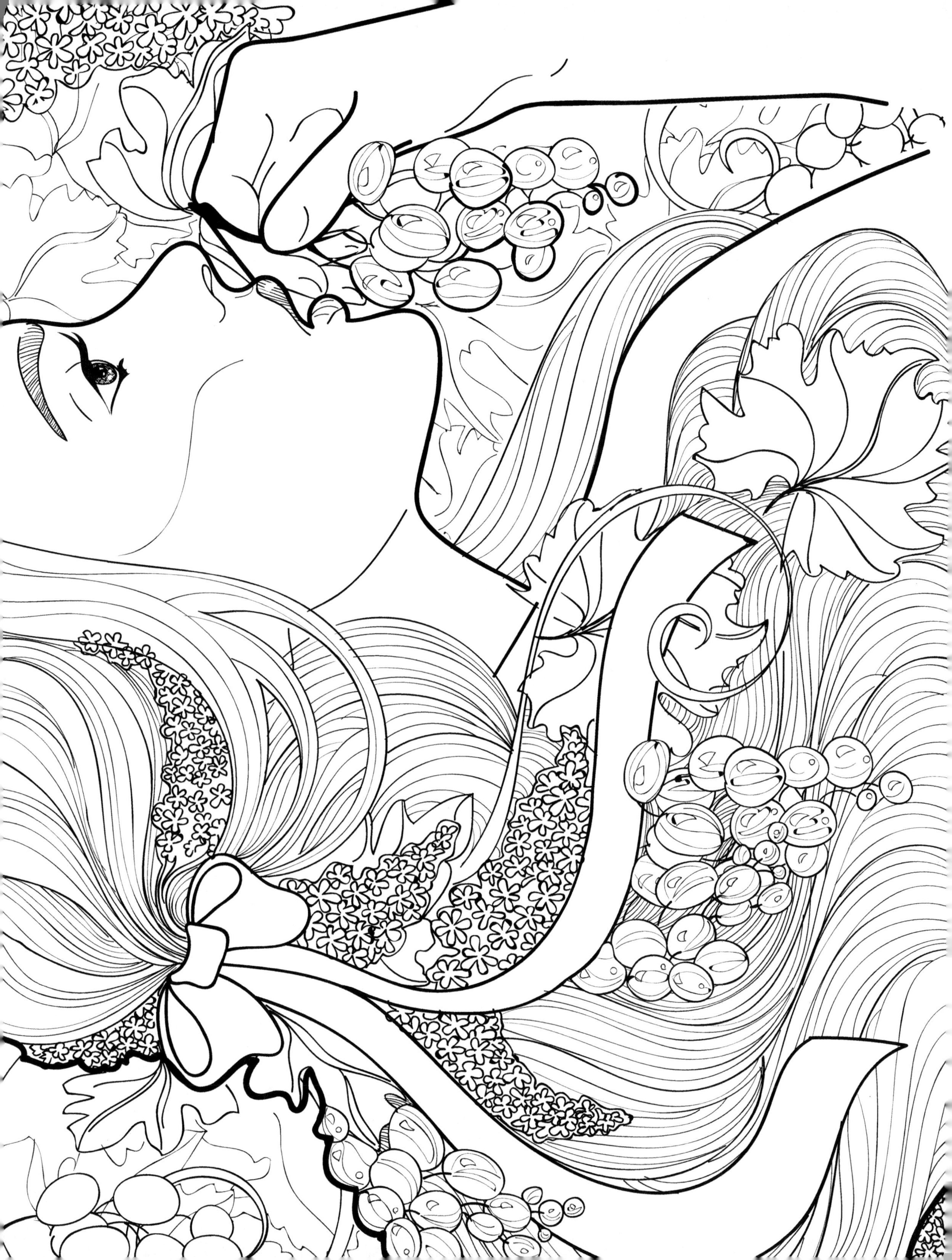

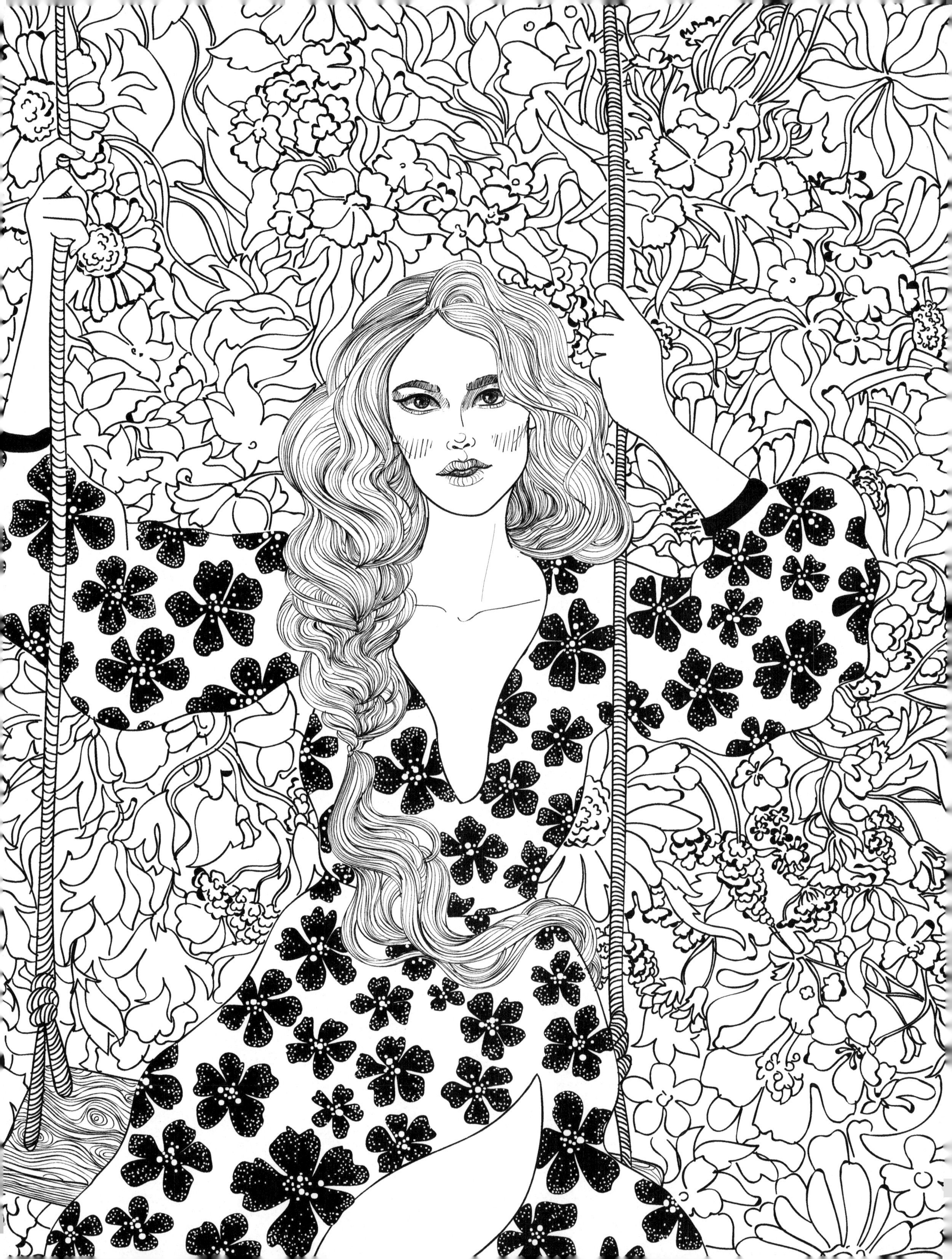

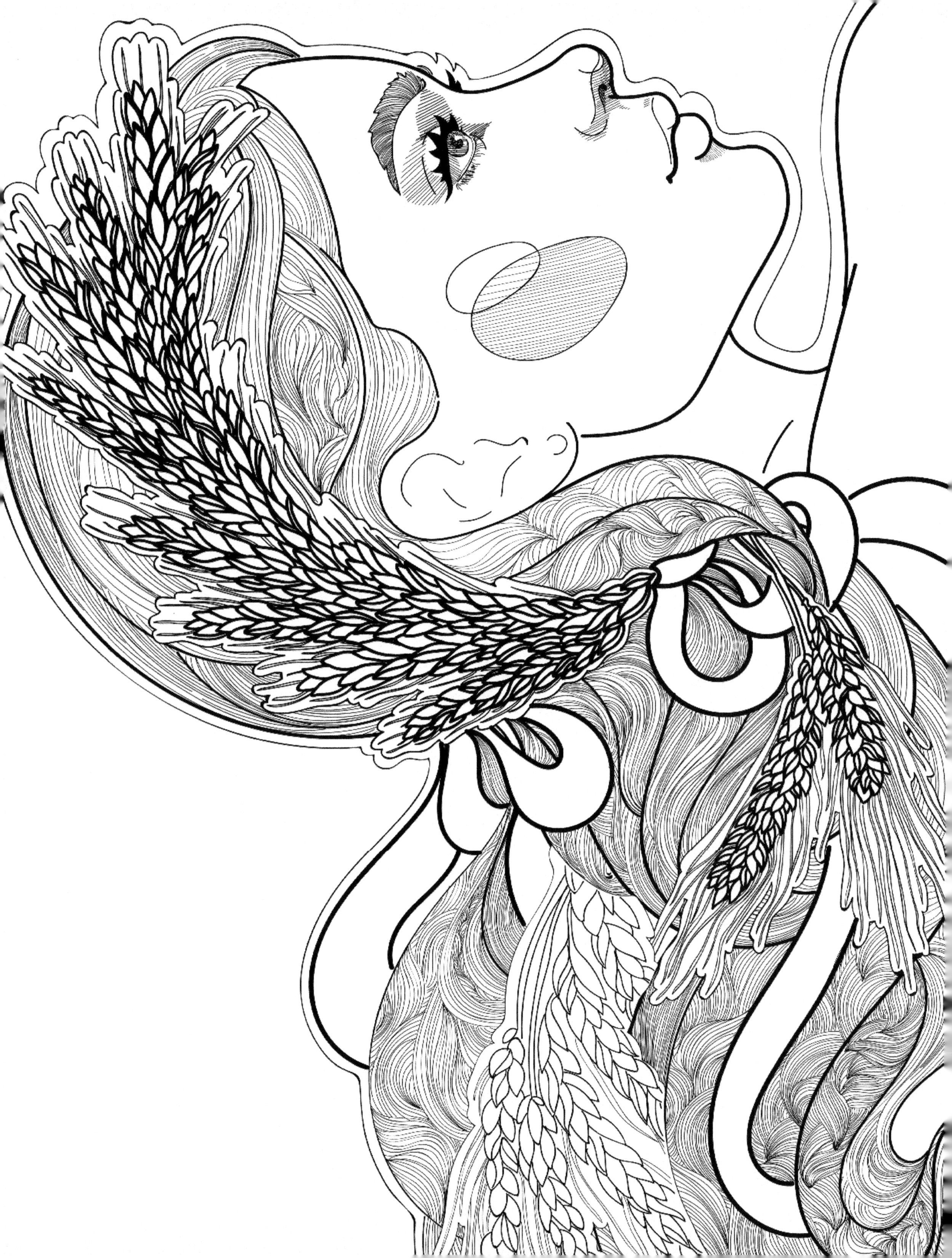

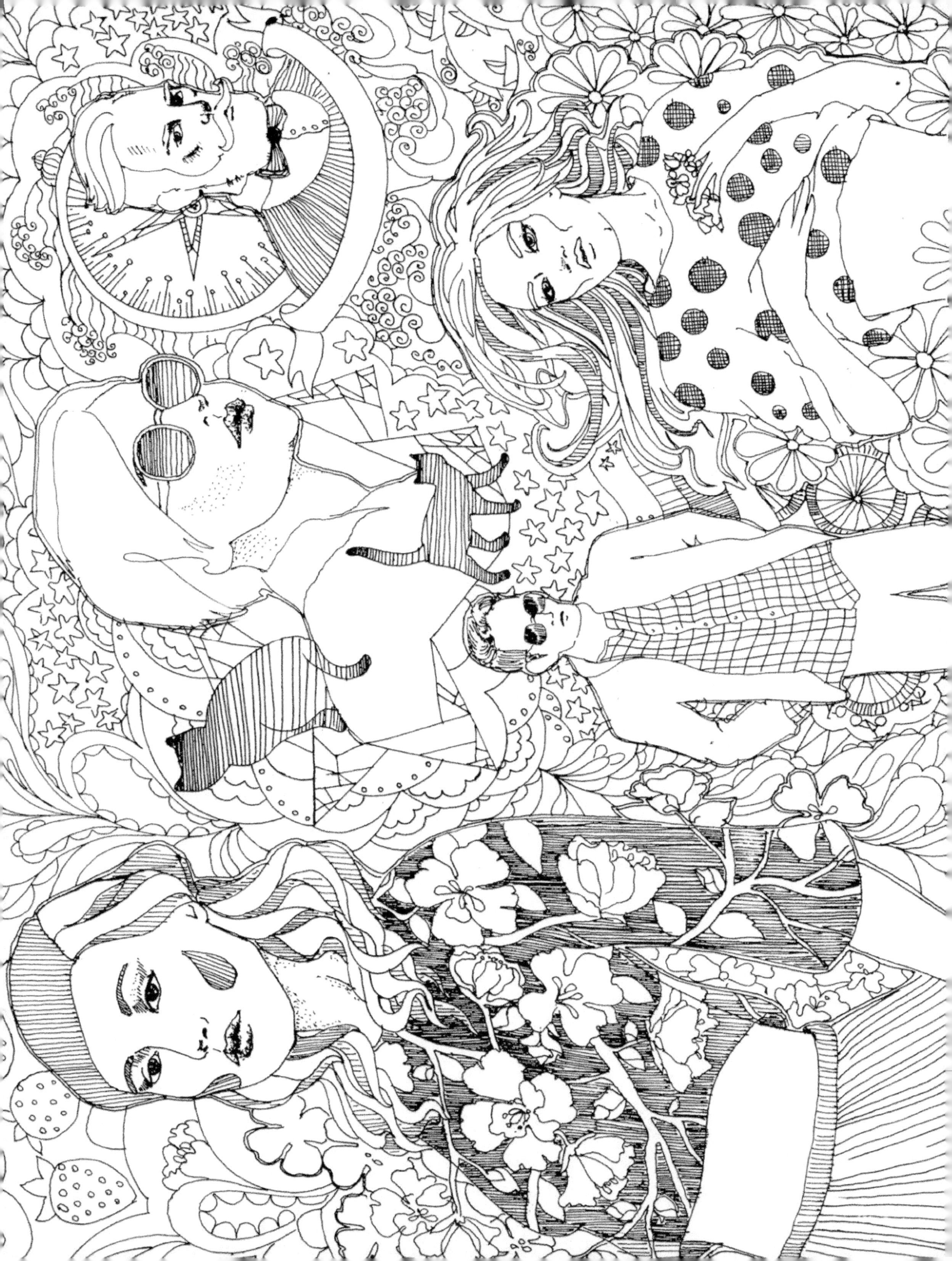

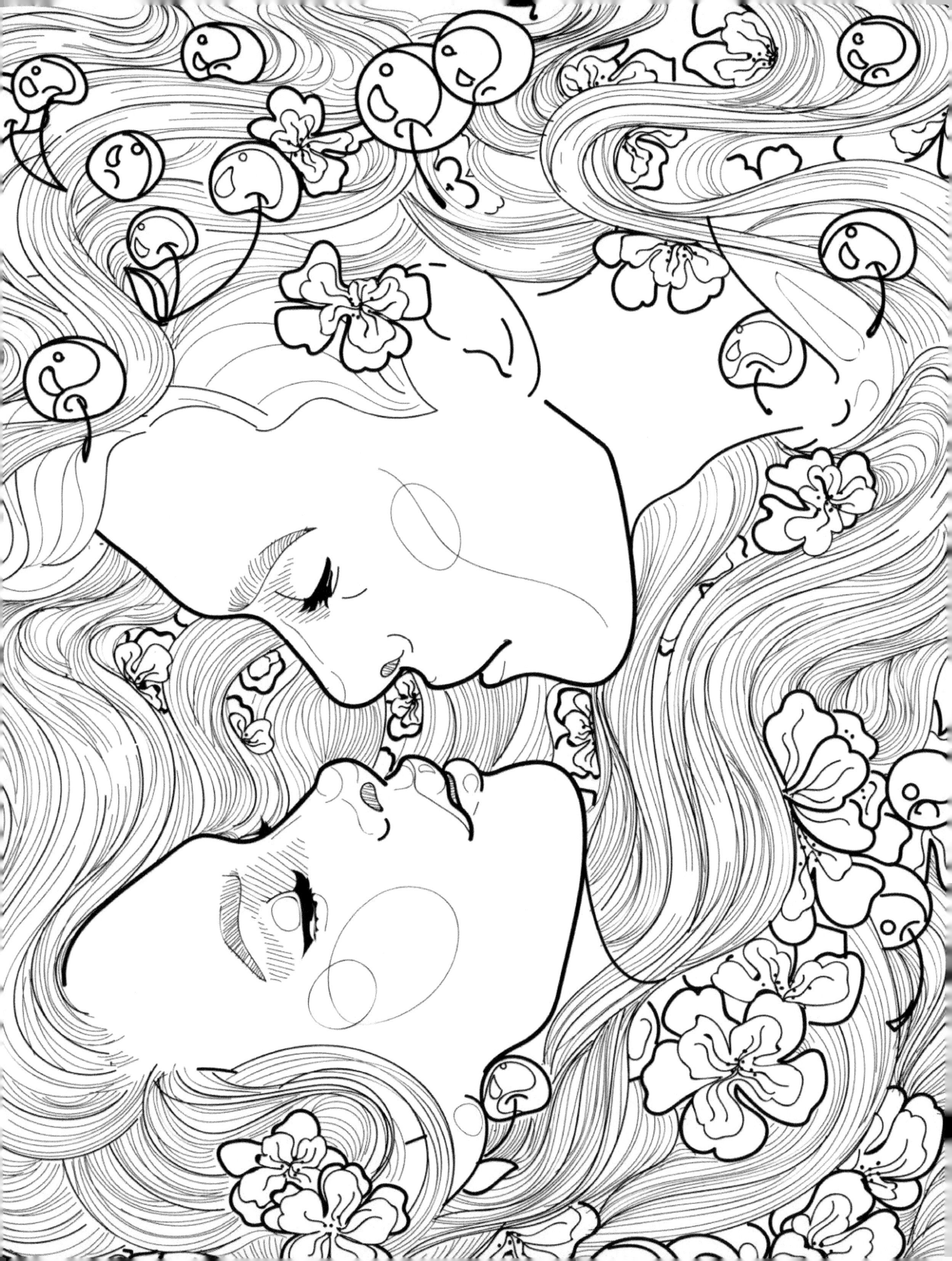

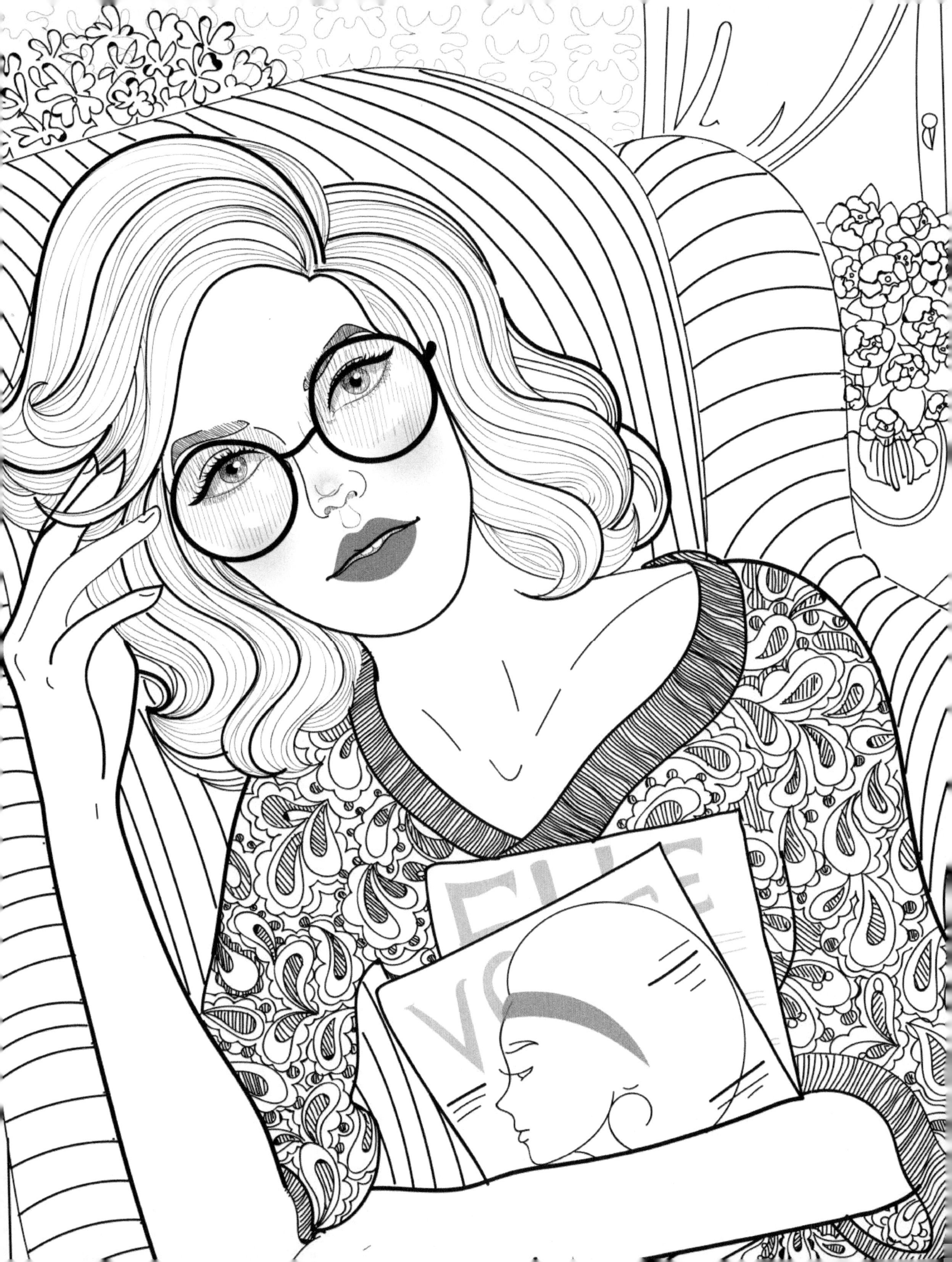
ELLE
VOGUE

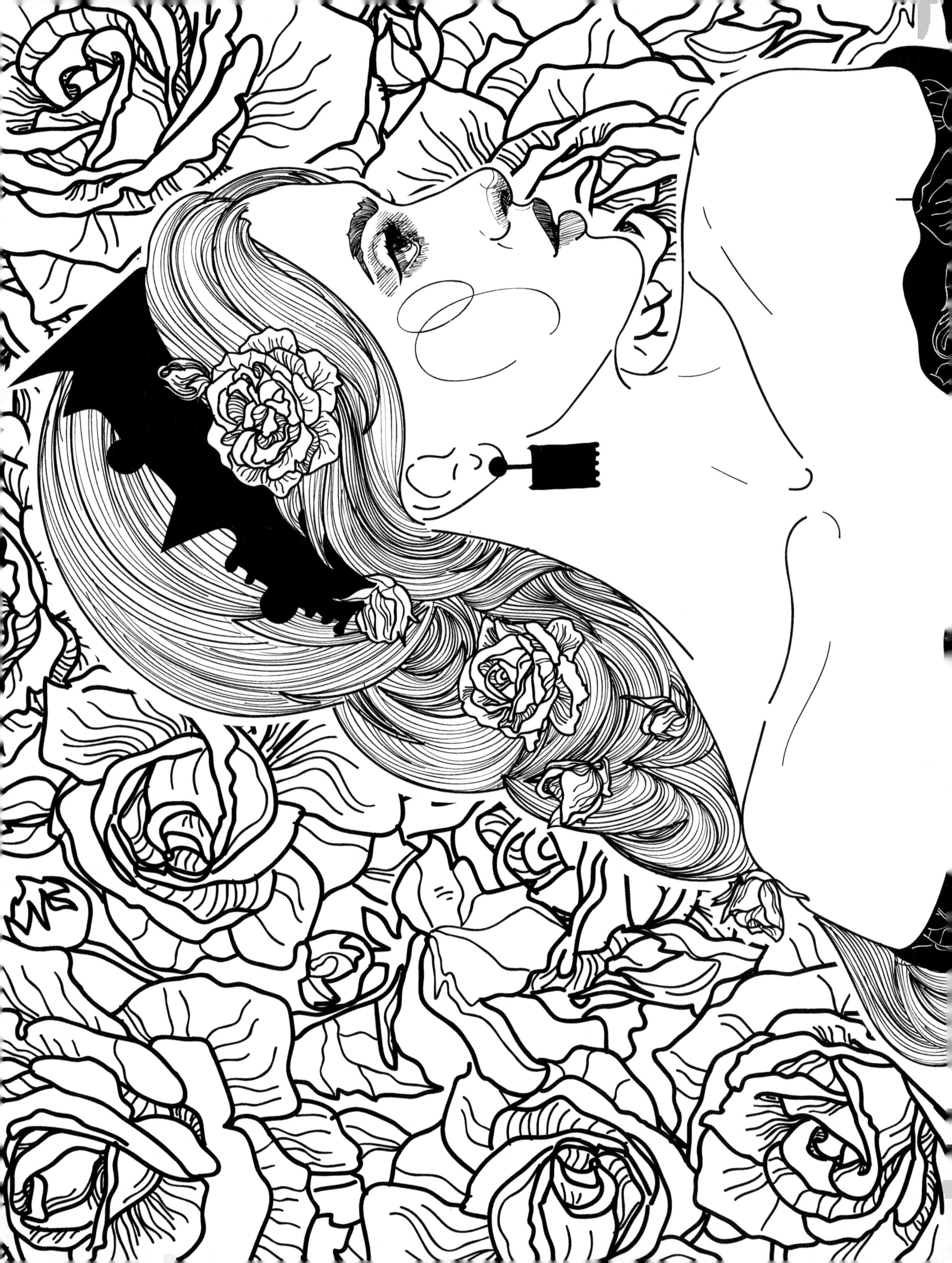

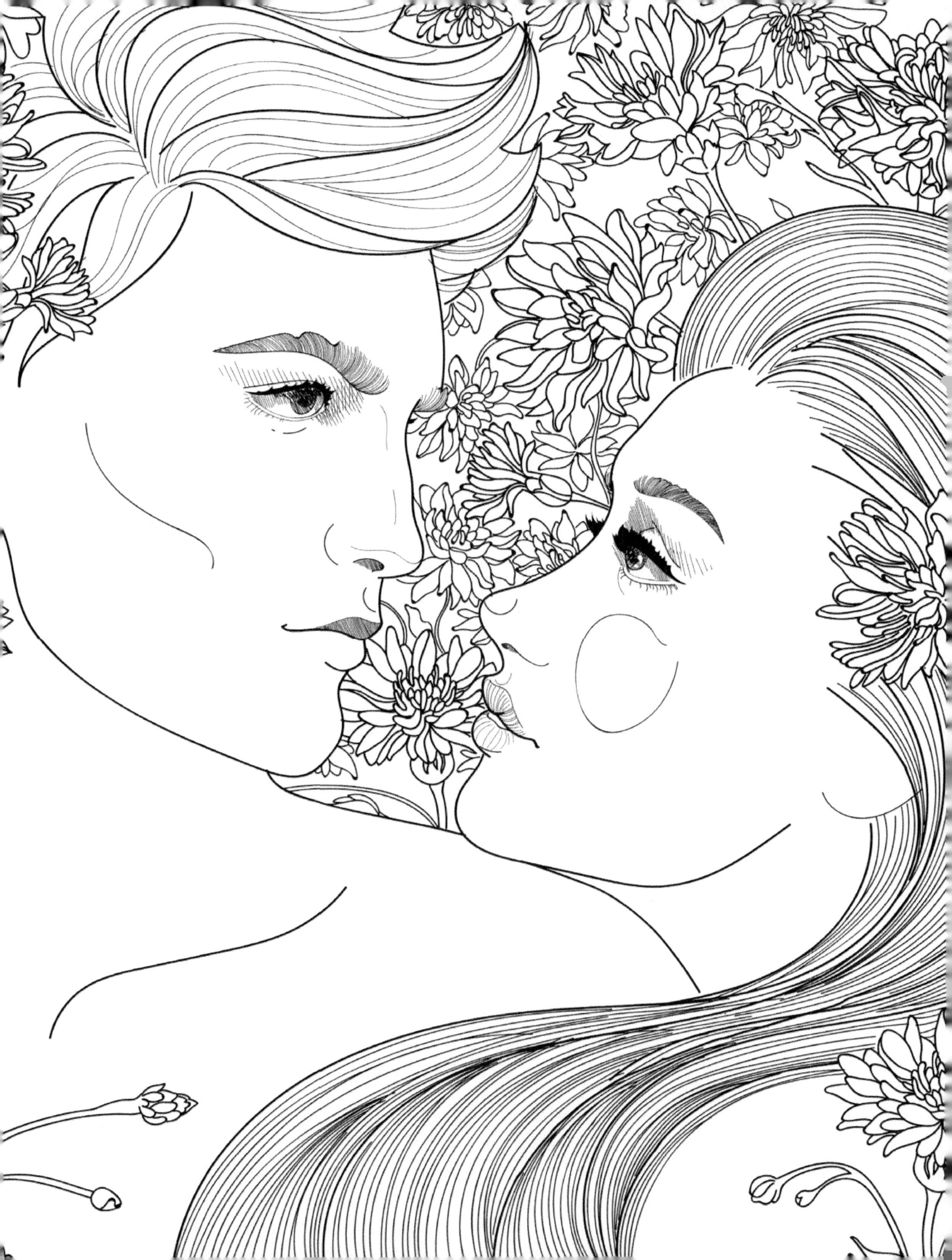

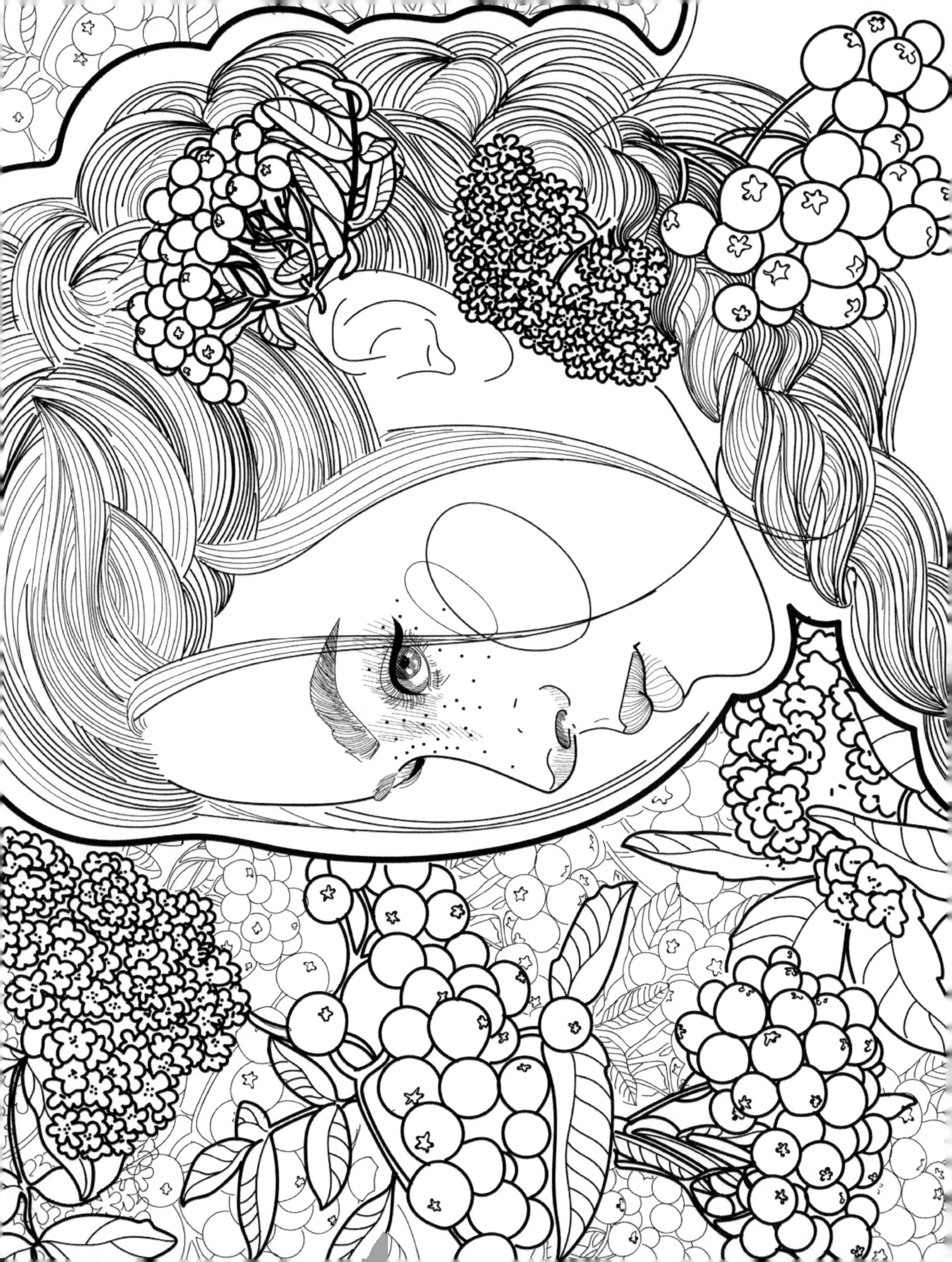

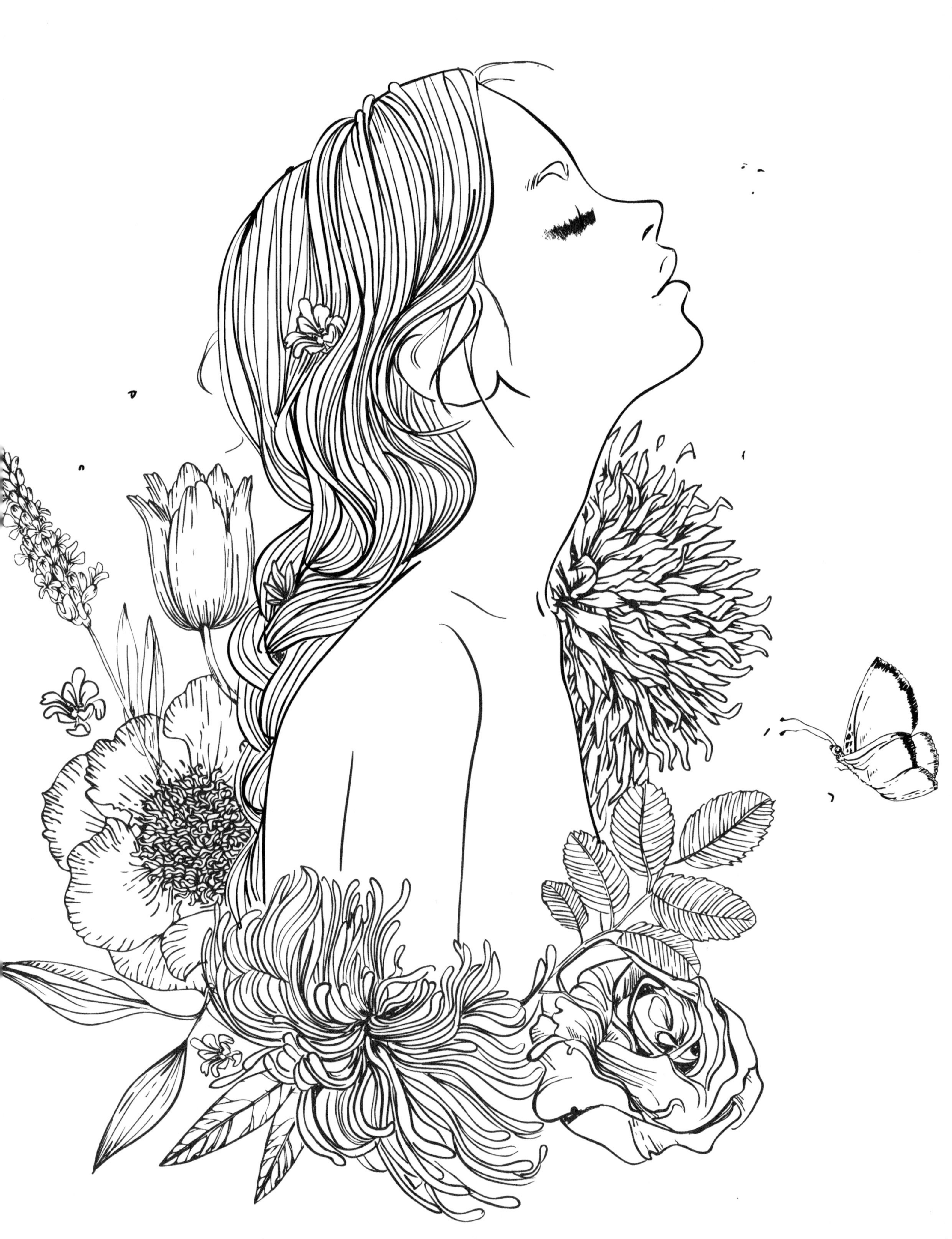

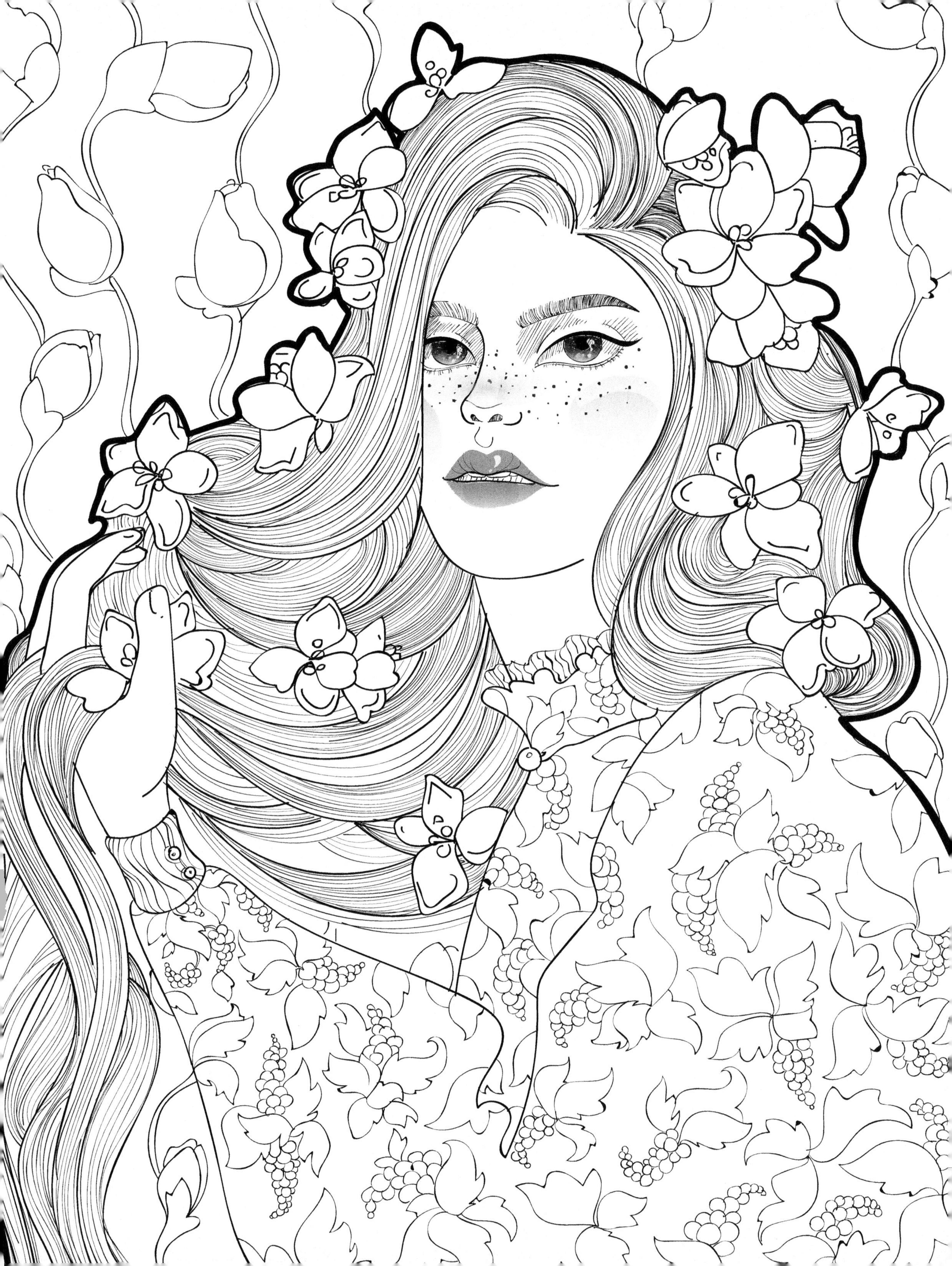

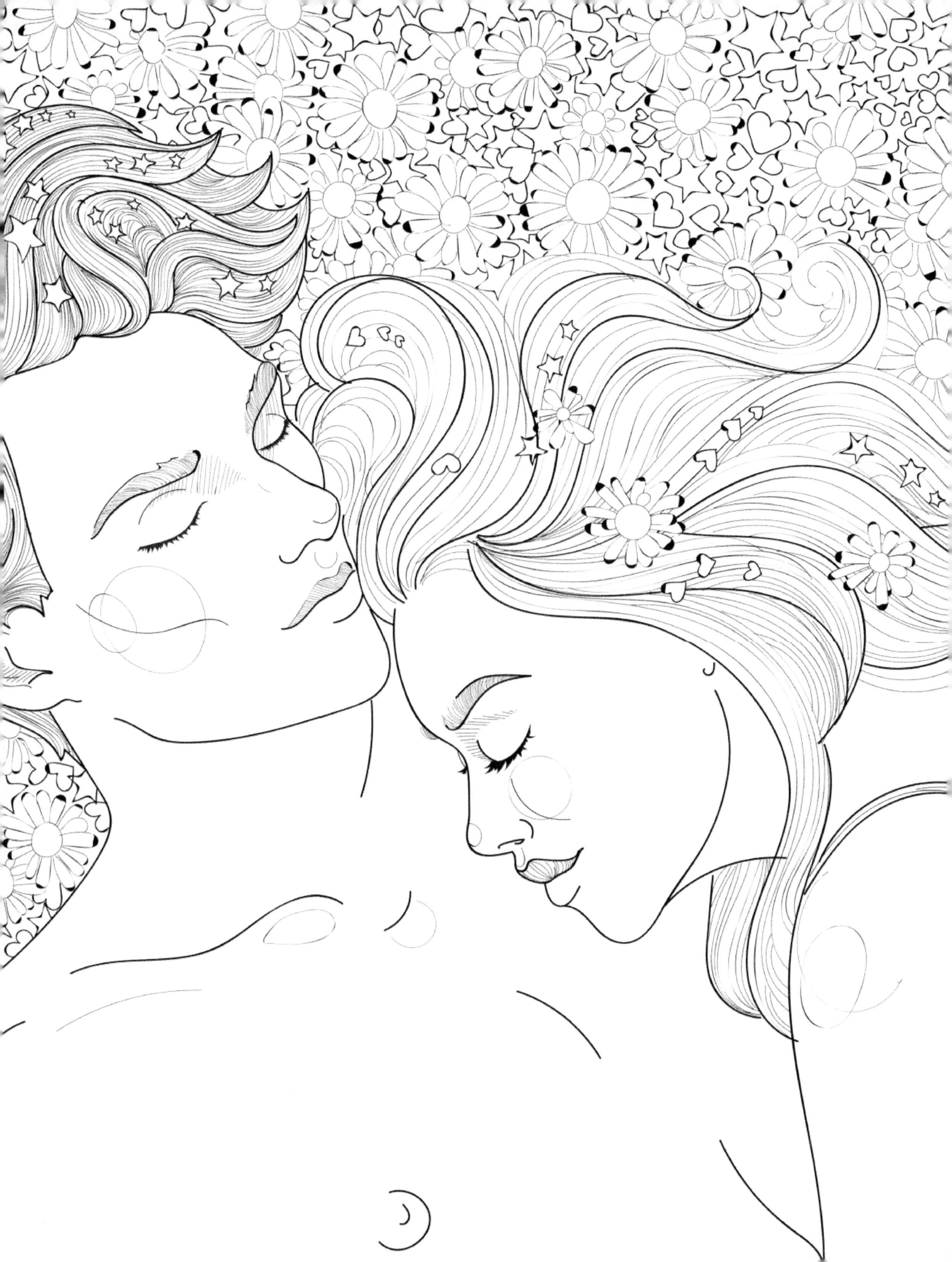

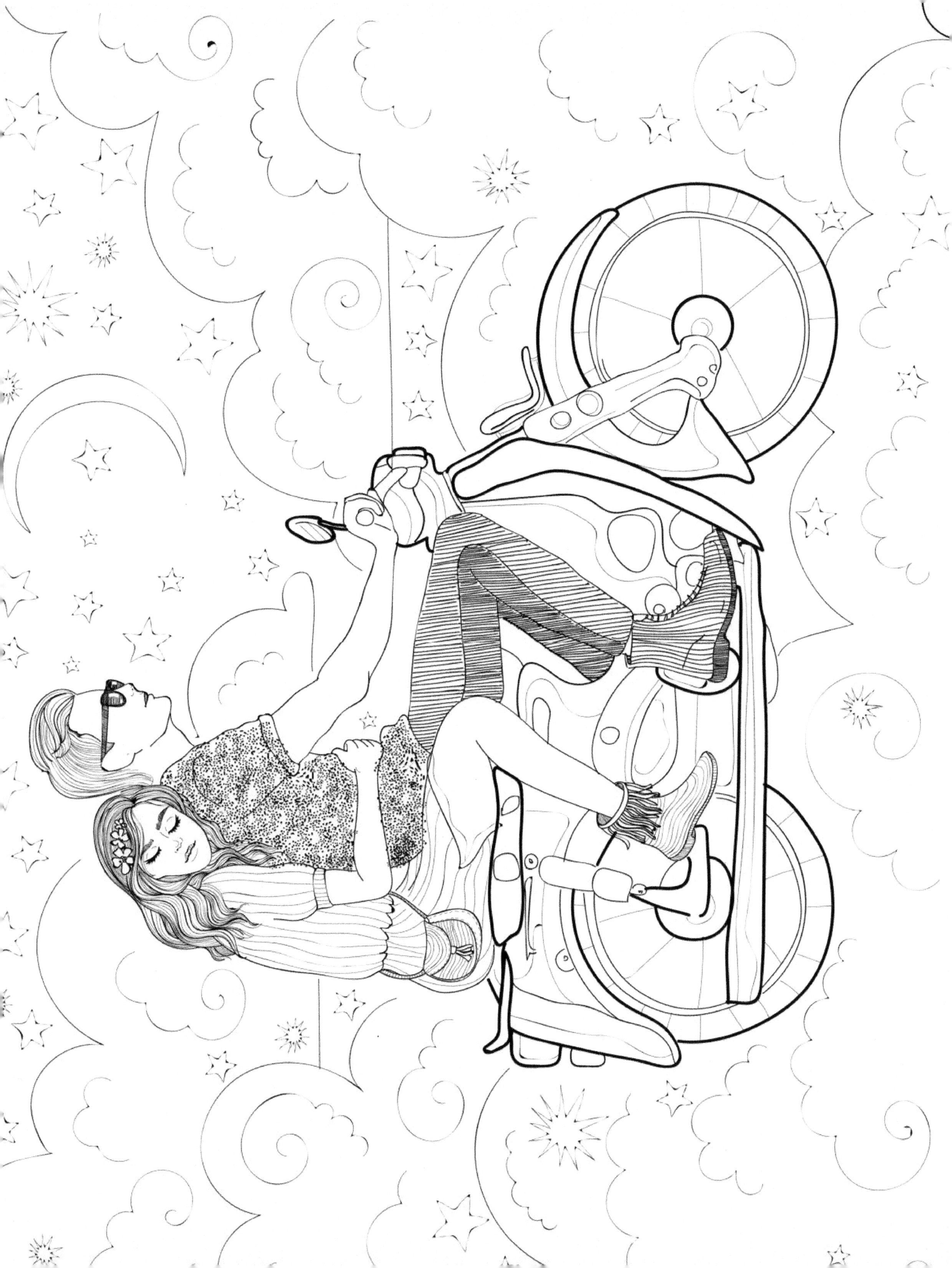

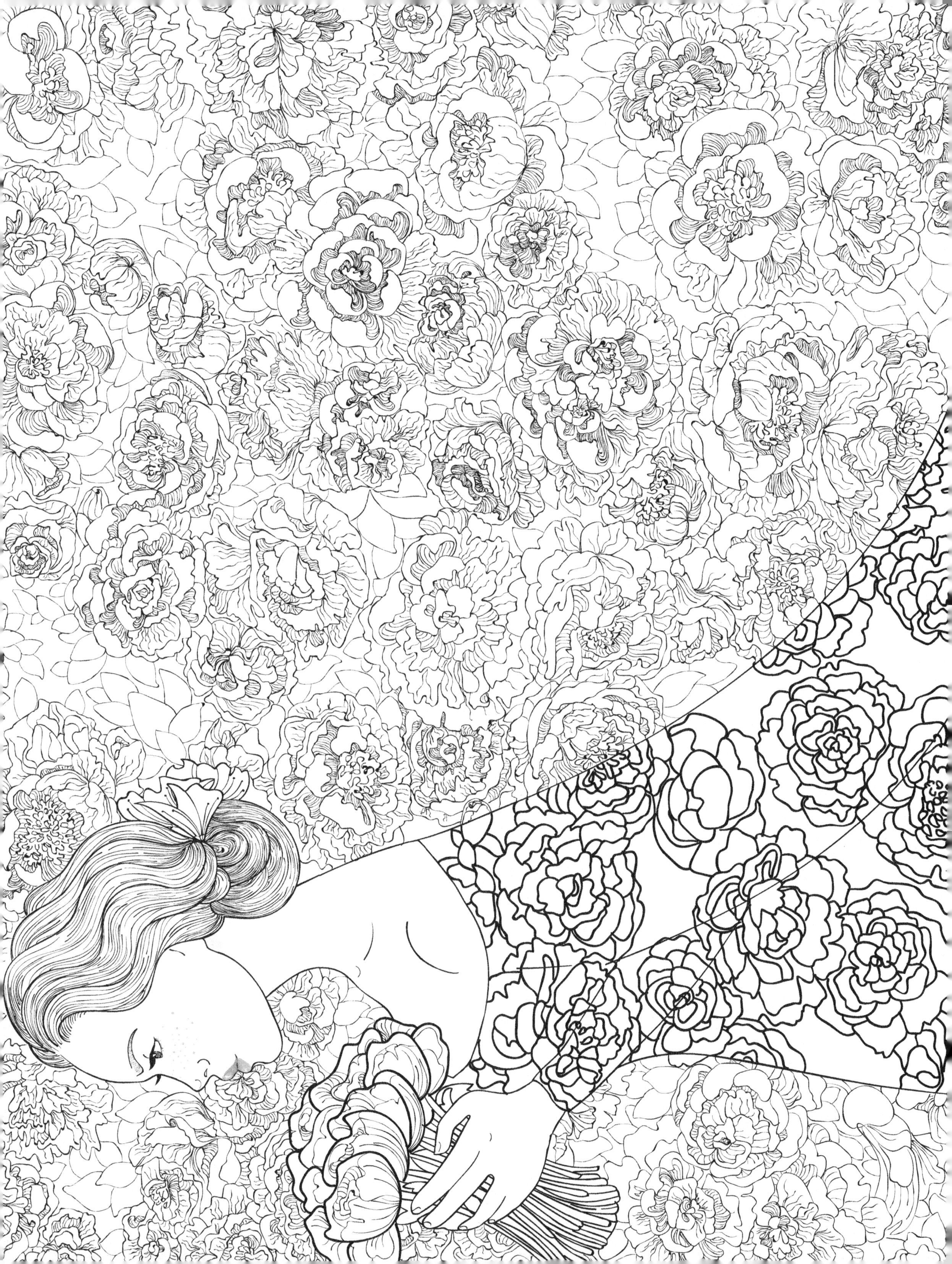

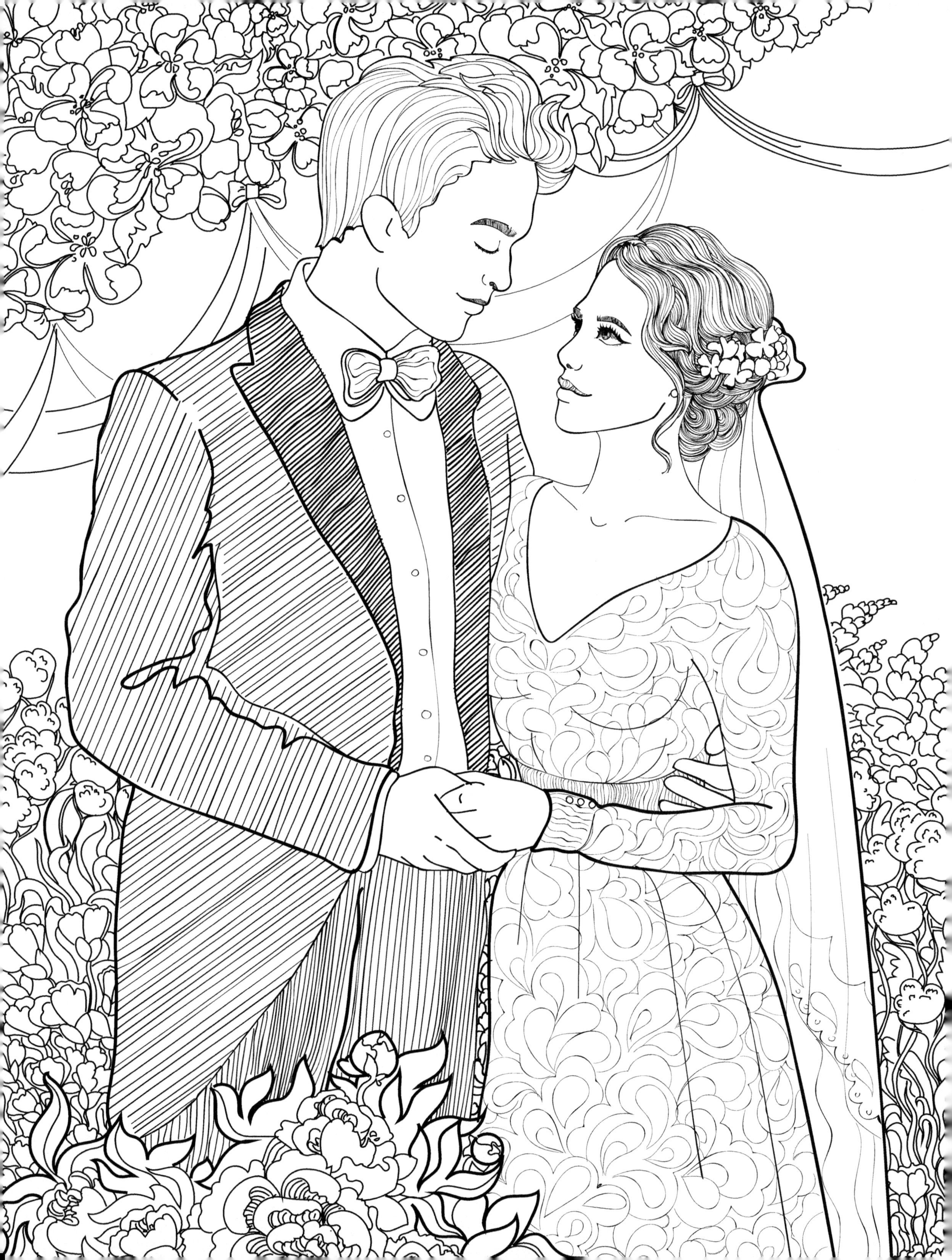

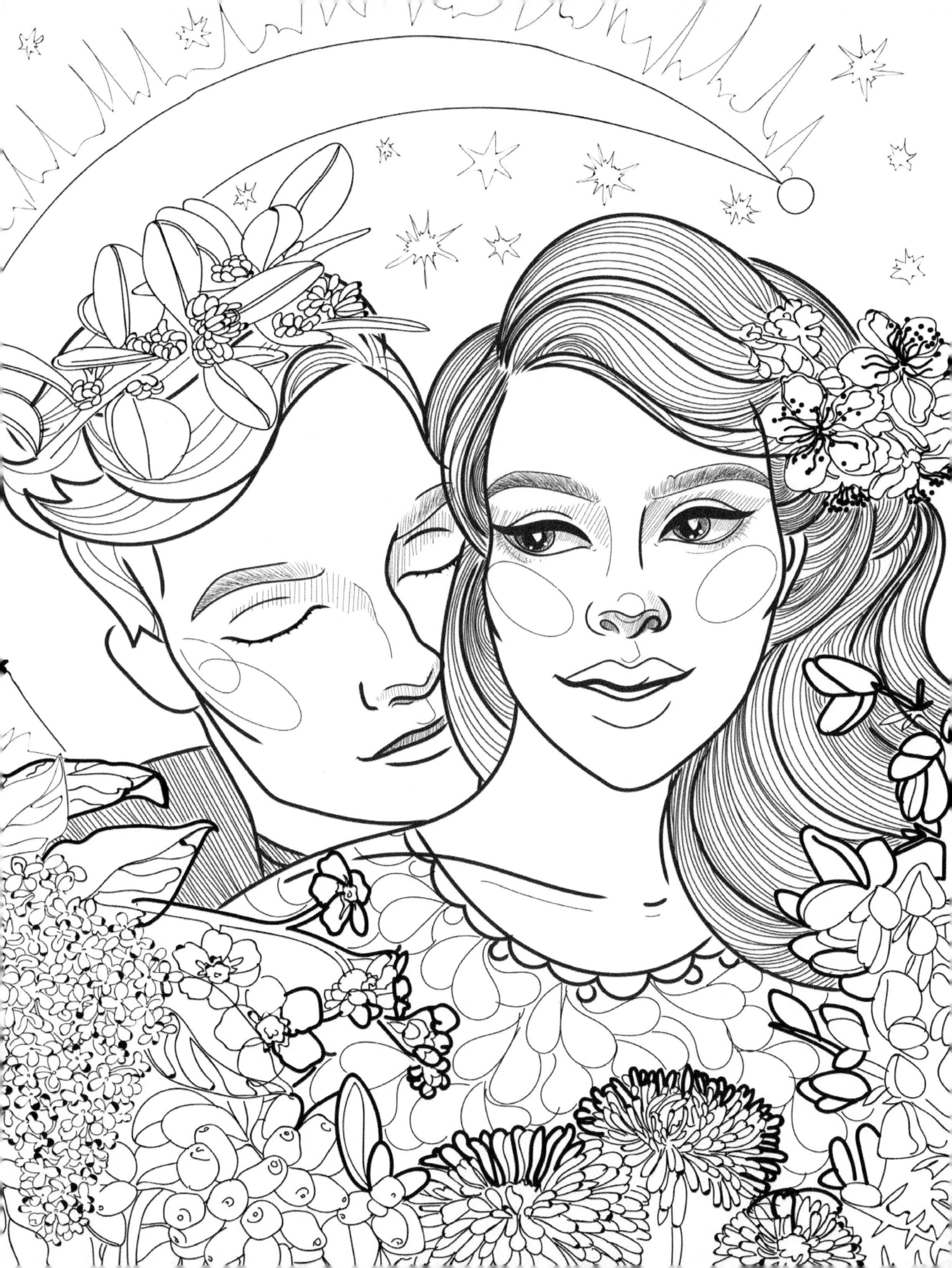

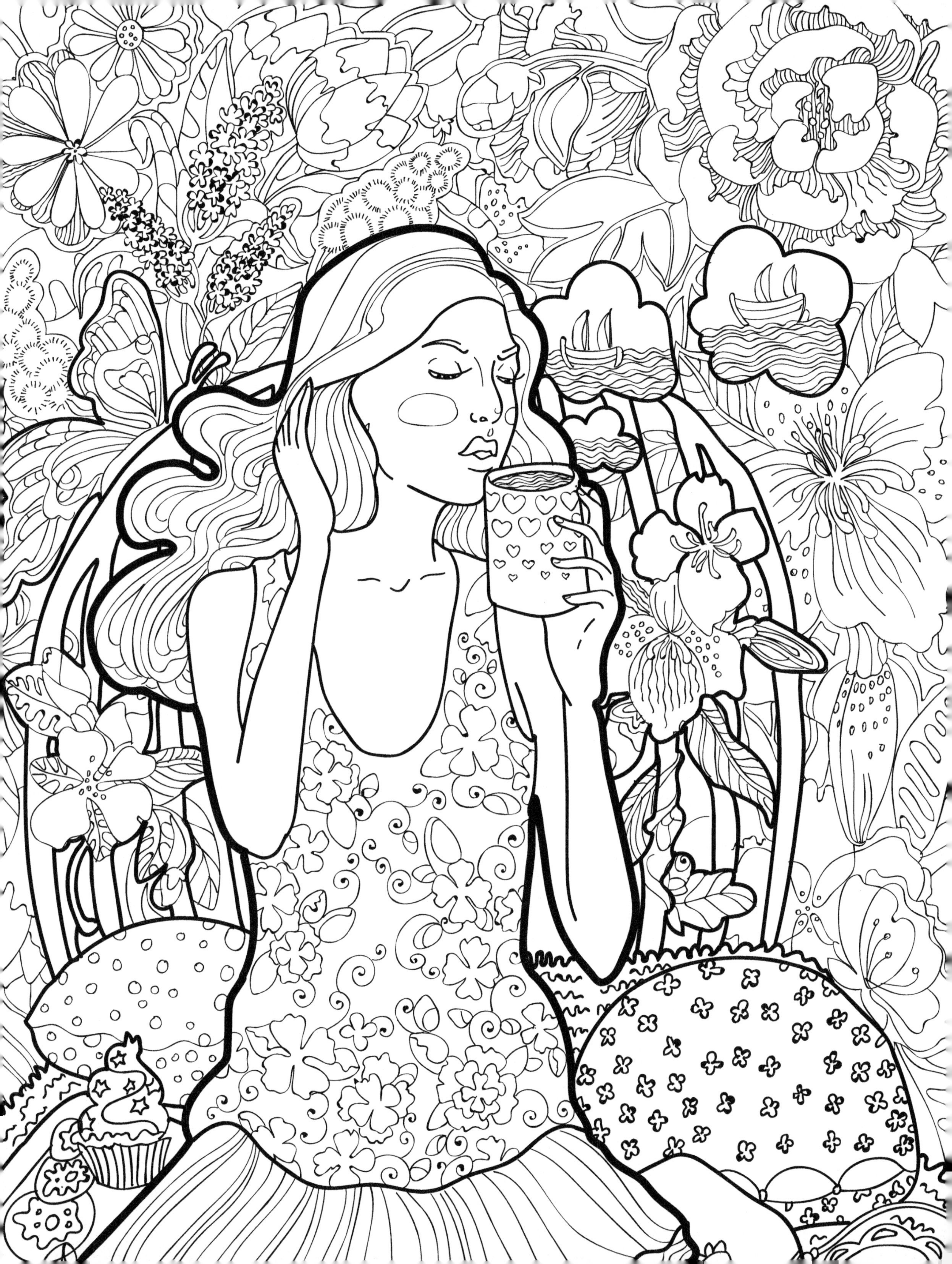

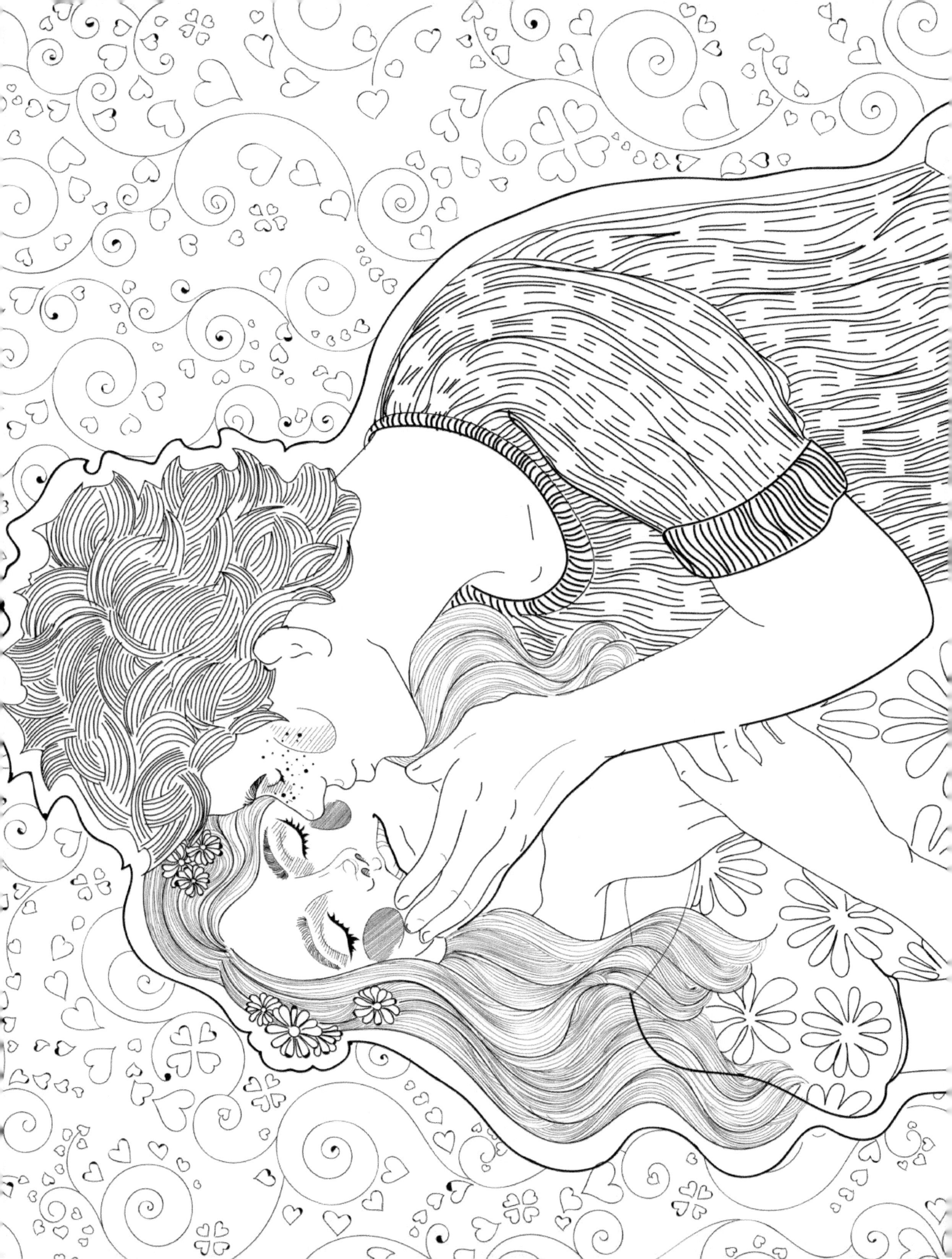

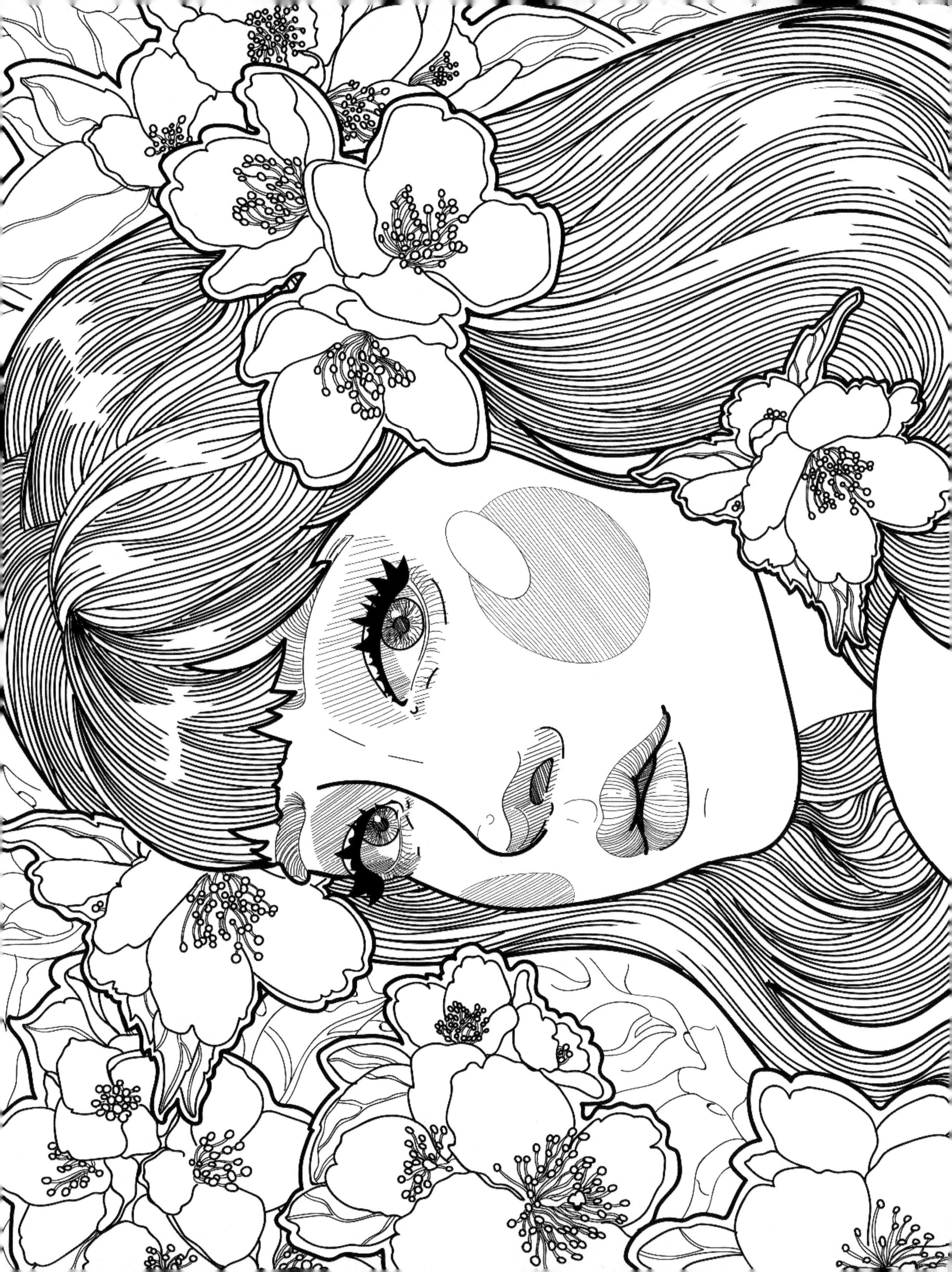

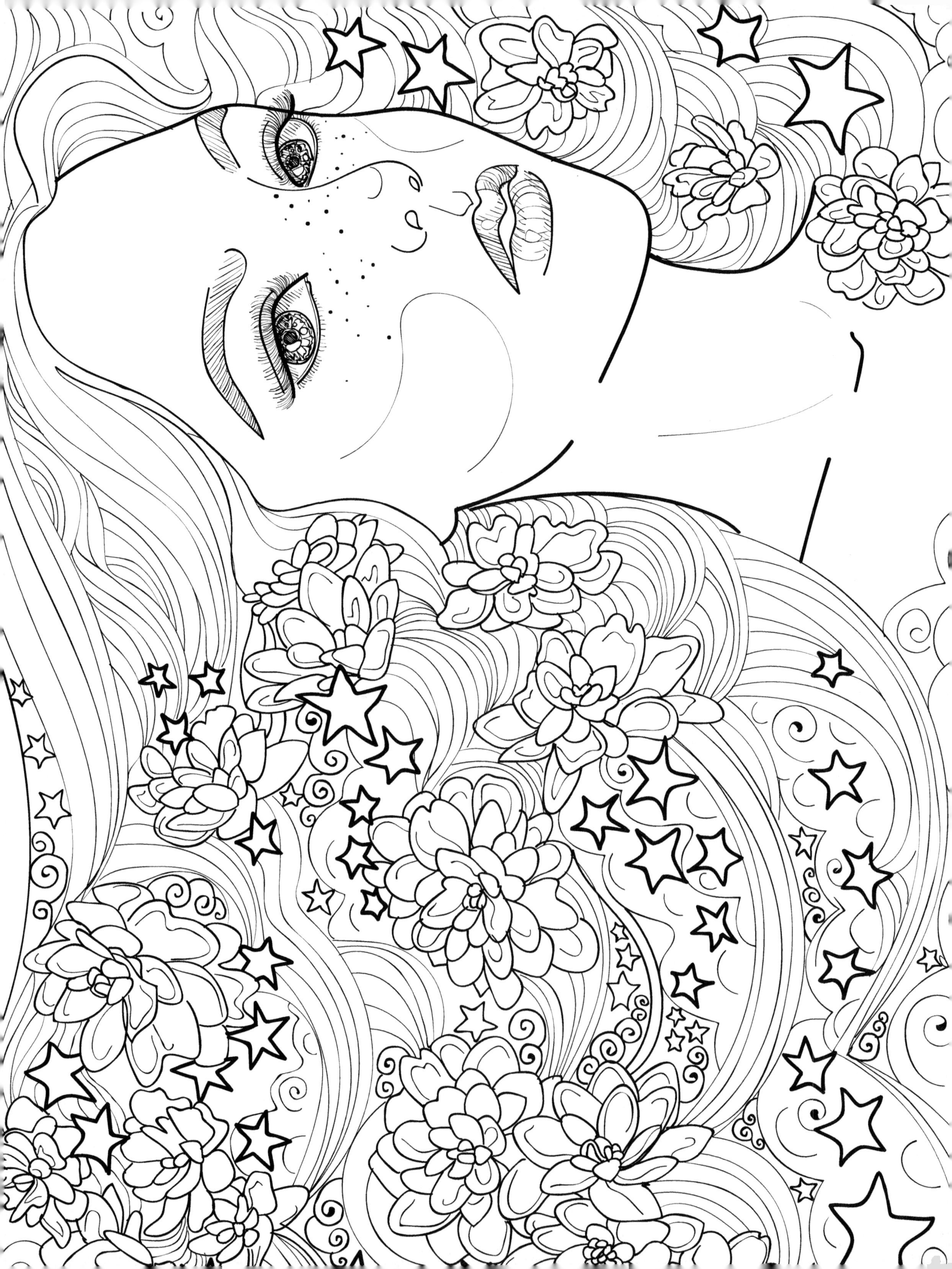

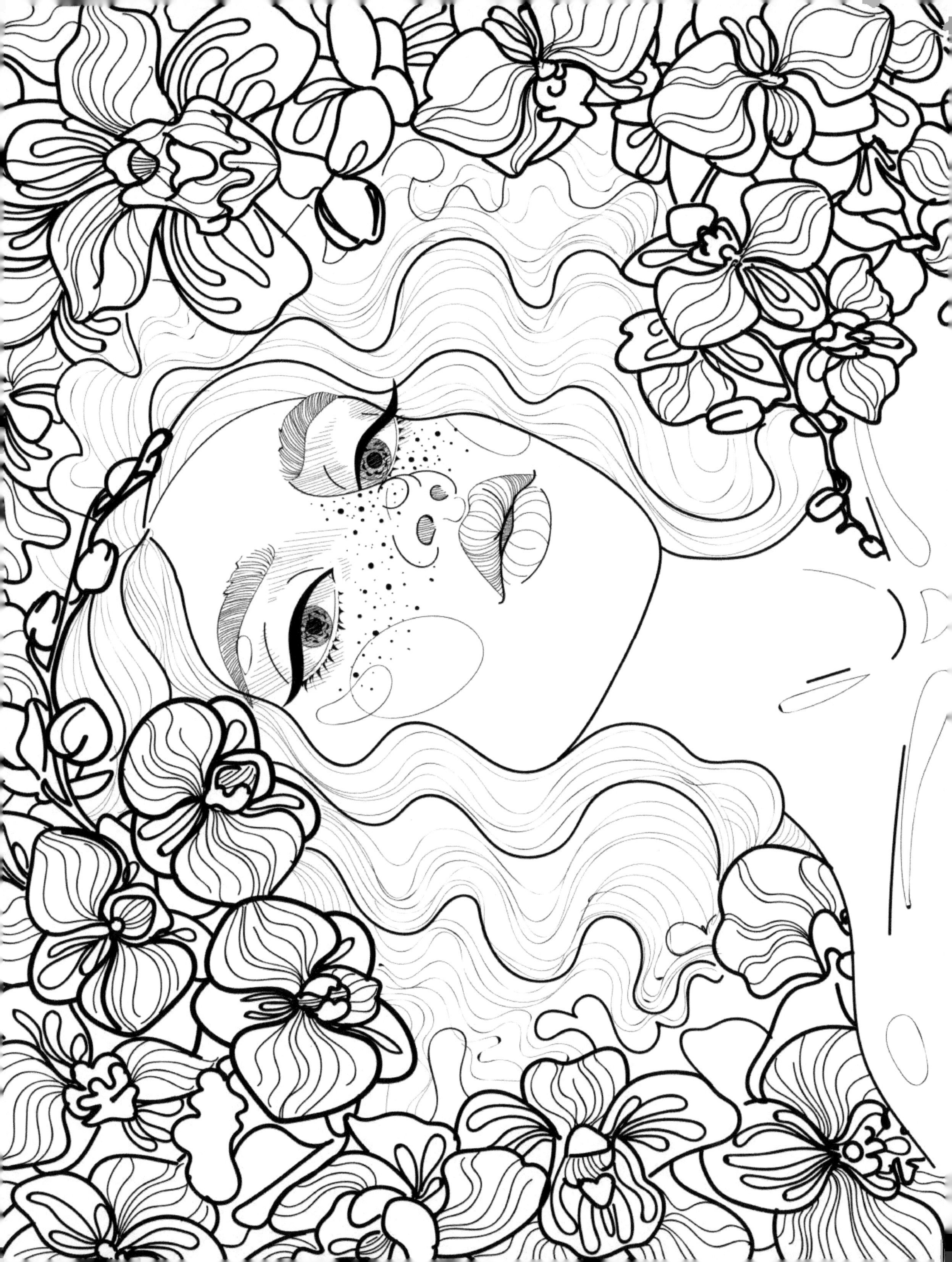

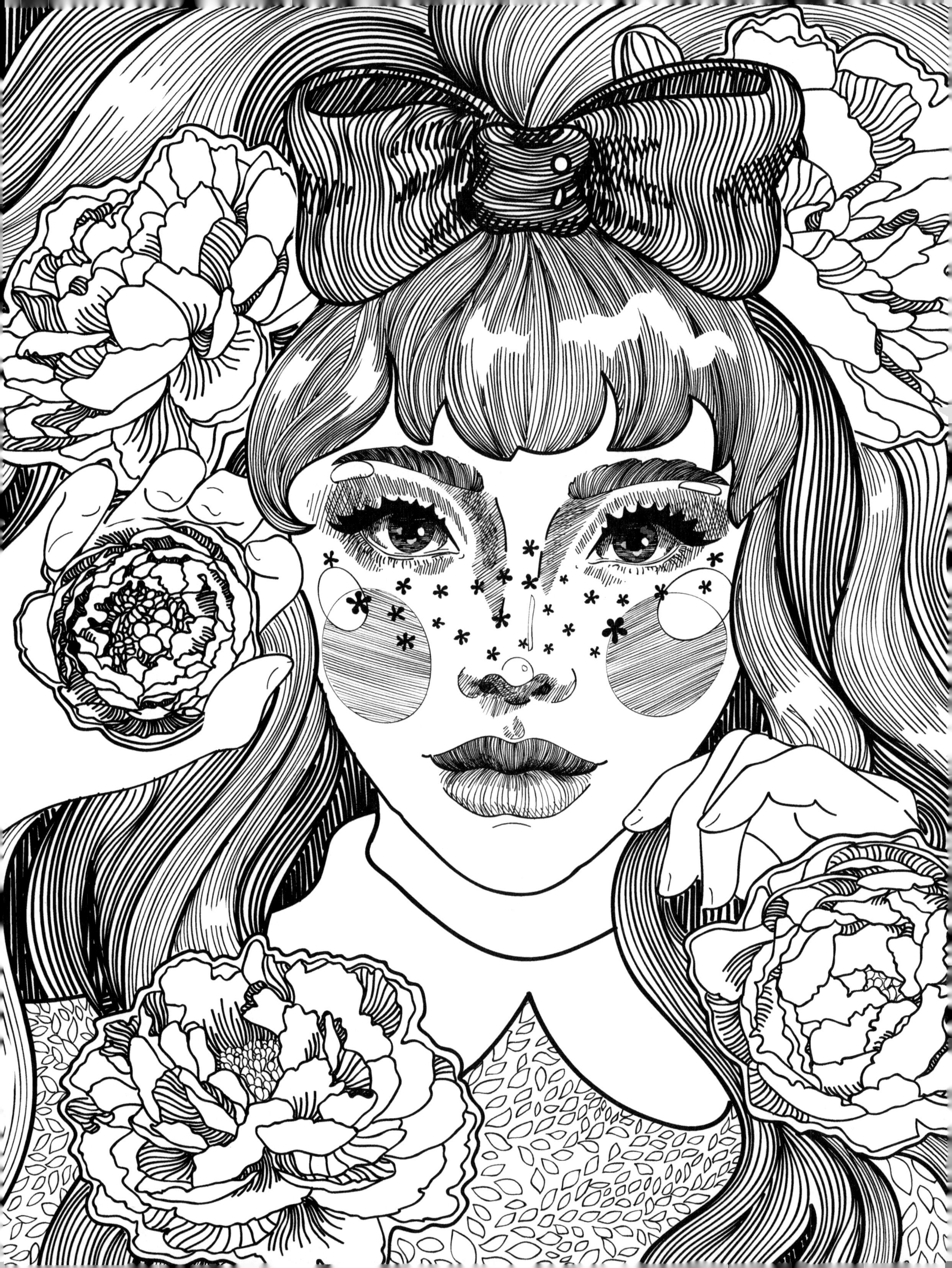

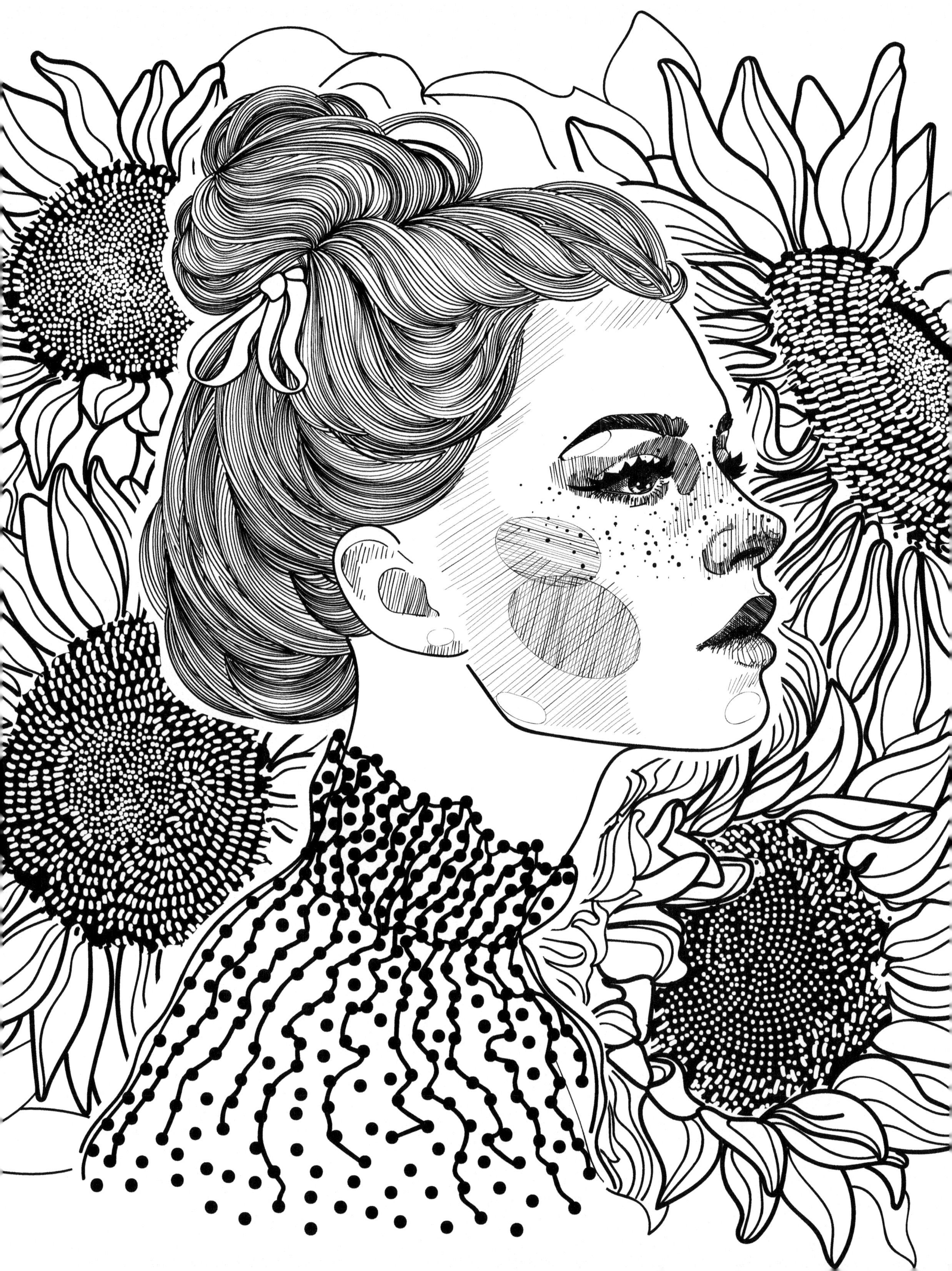

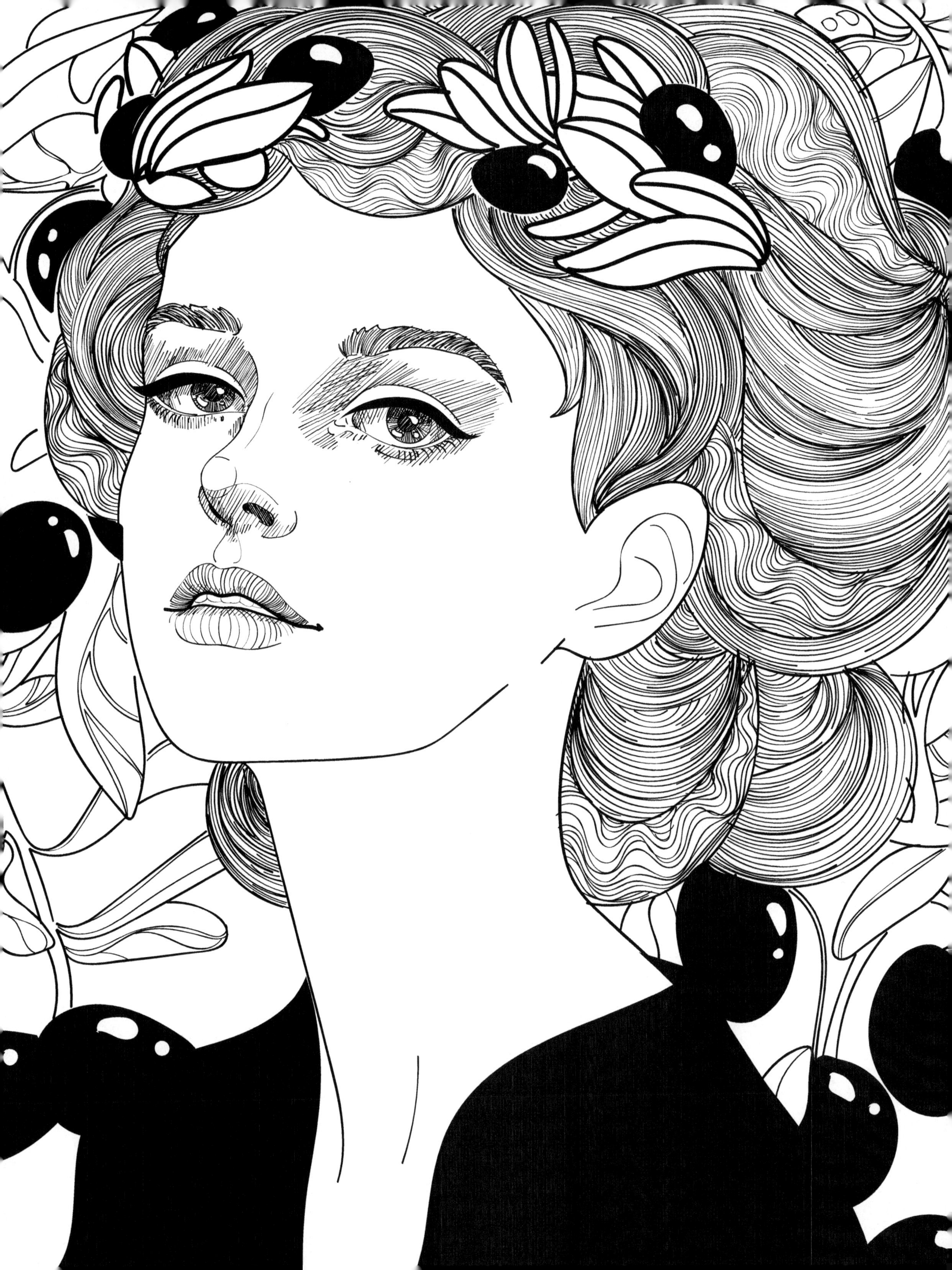

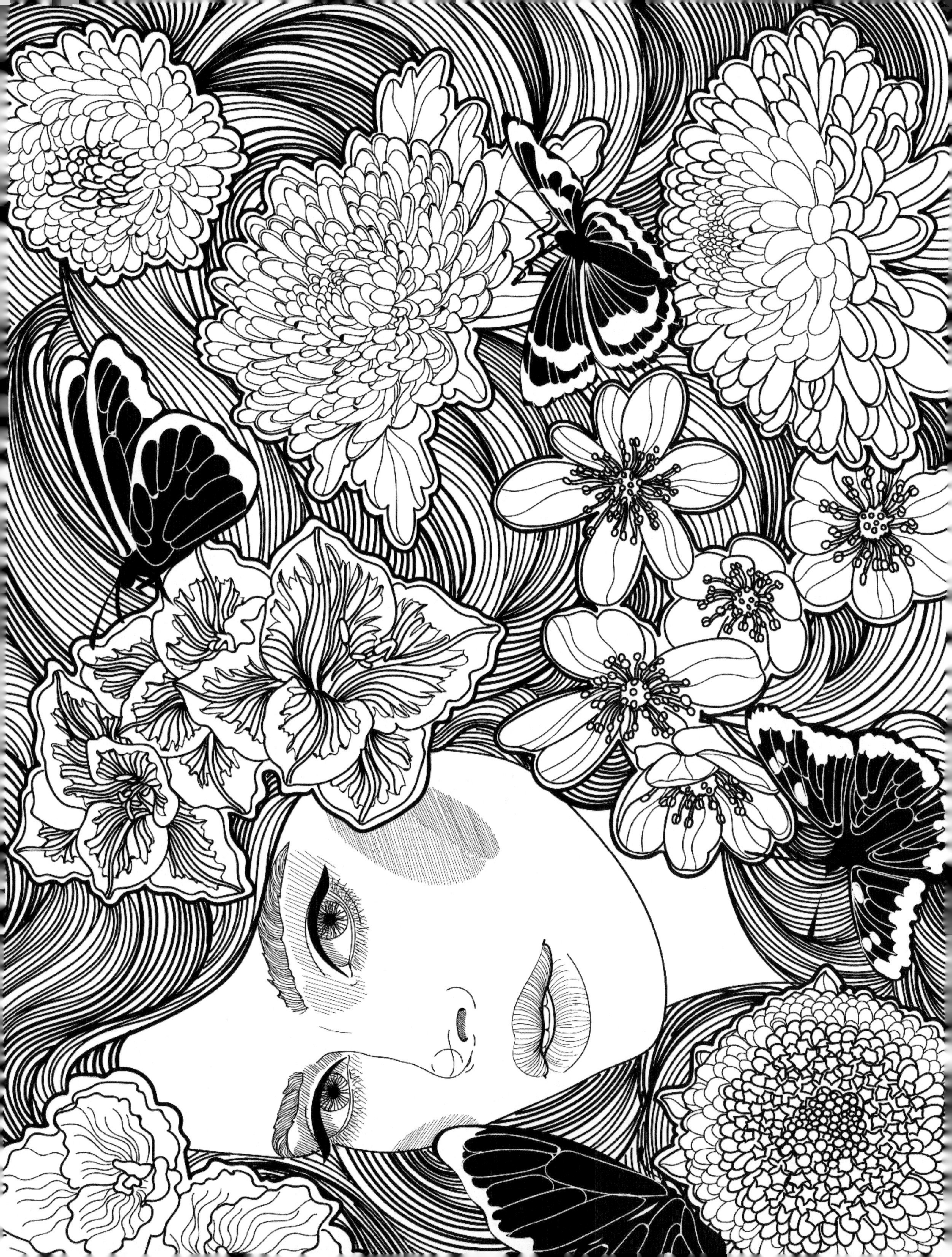

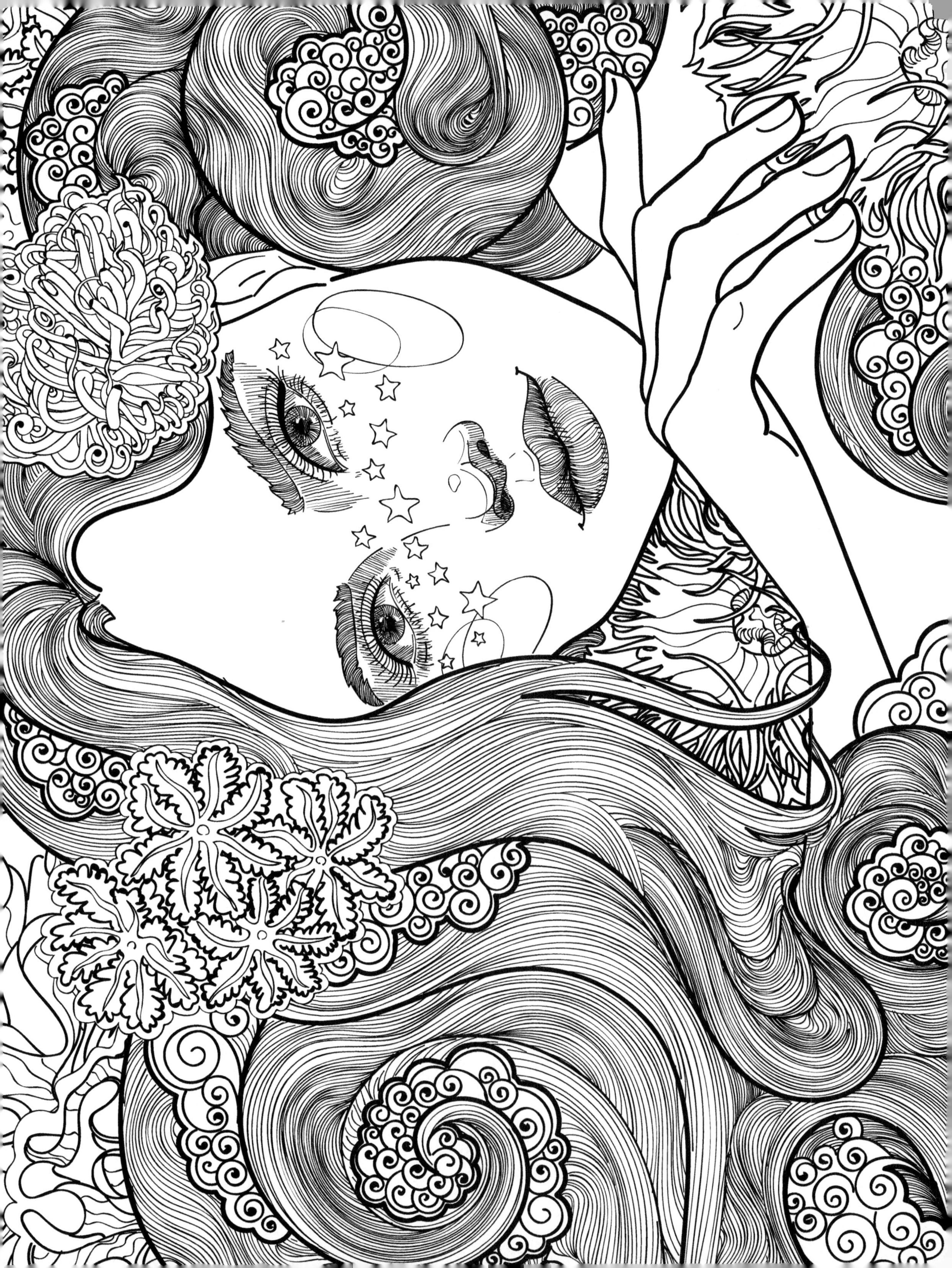

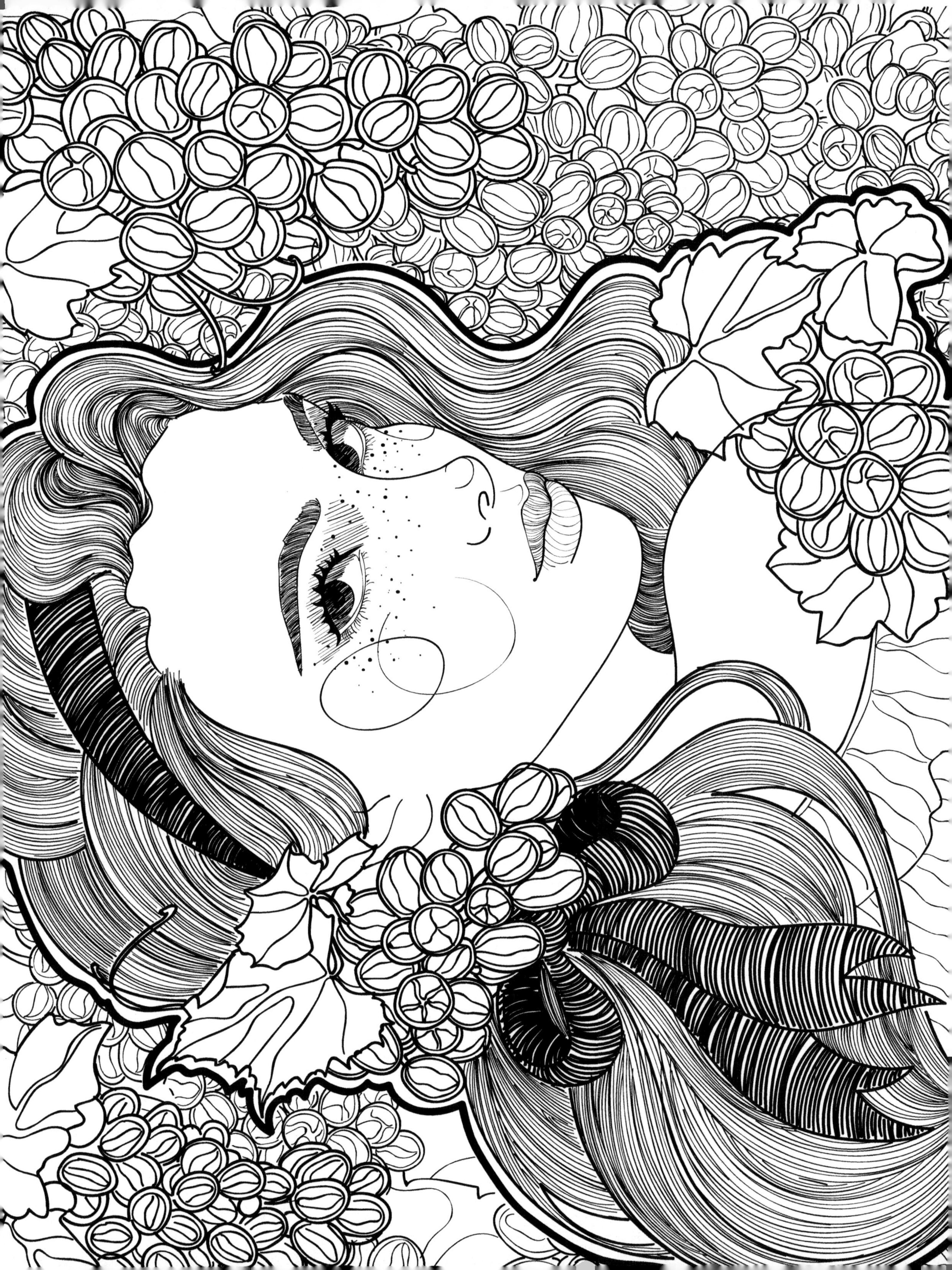

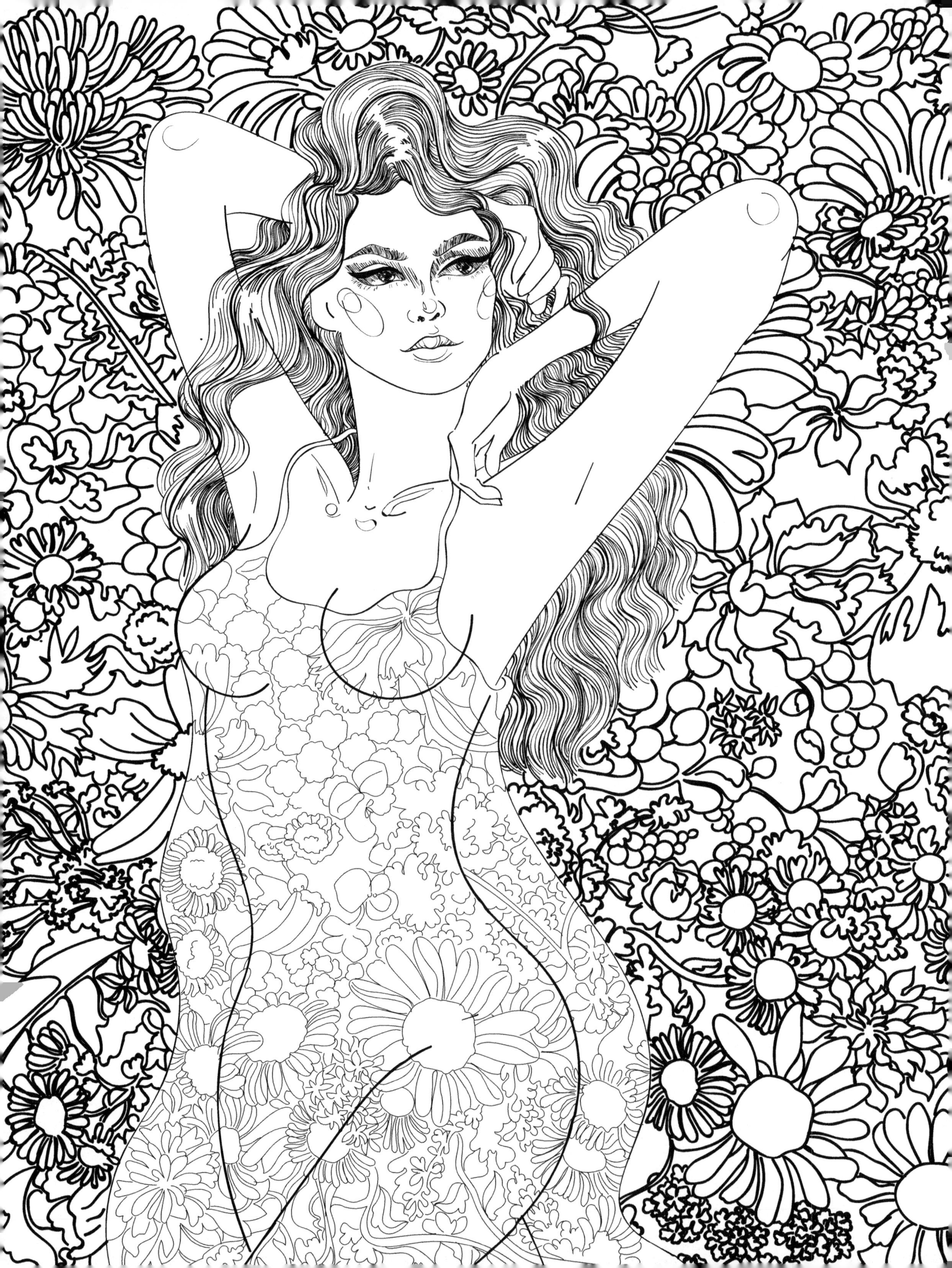

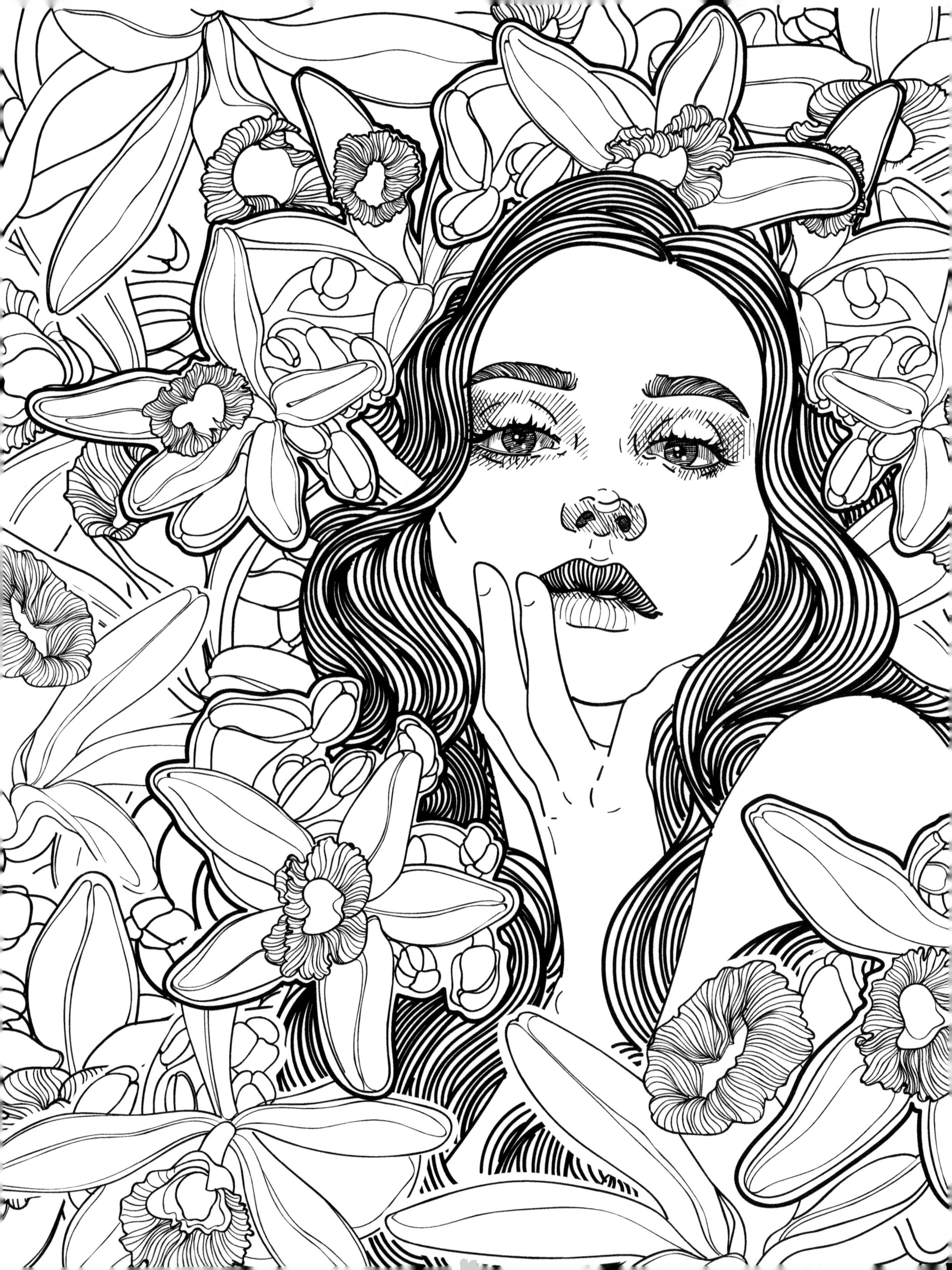

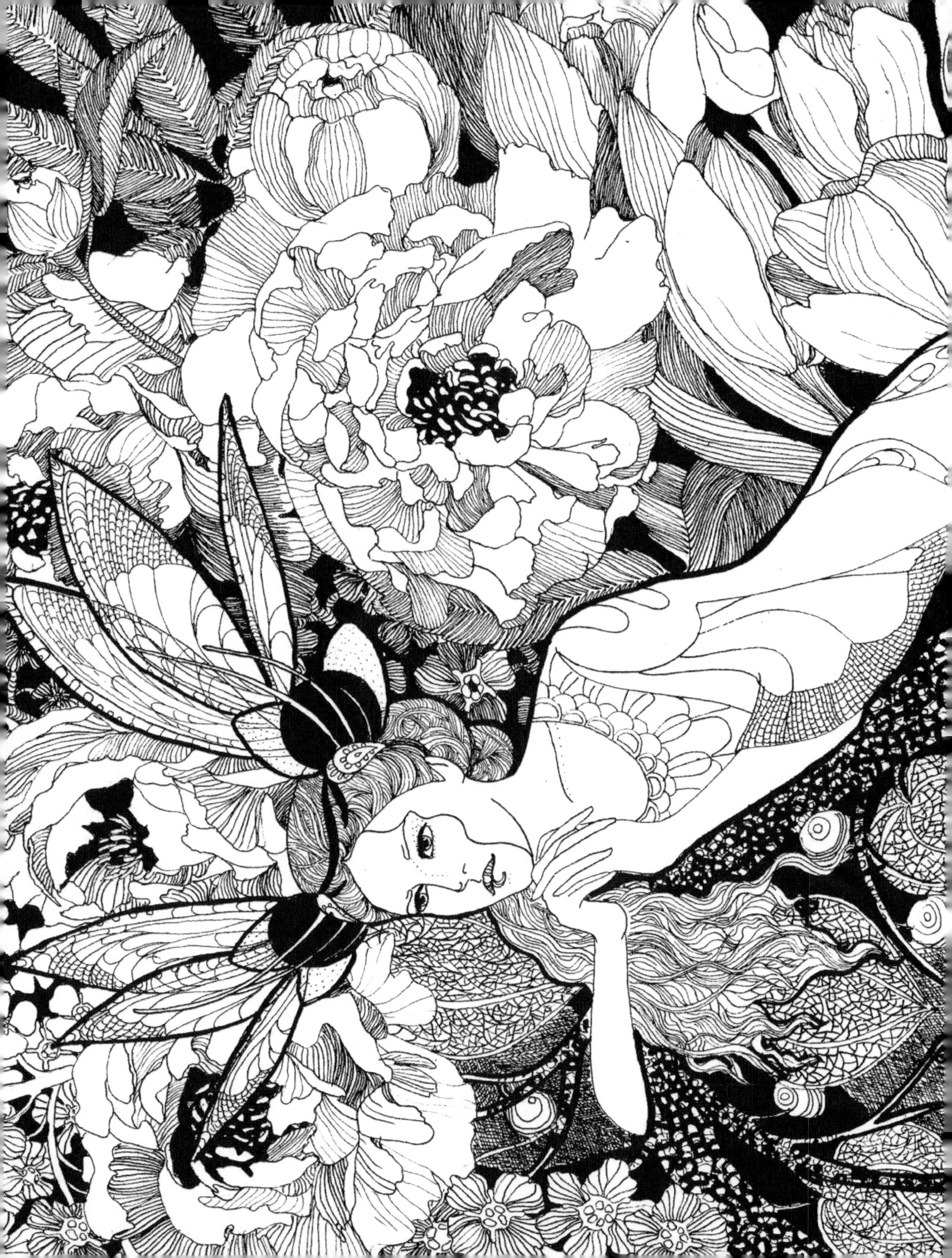

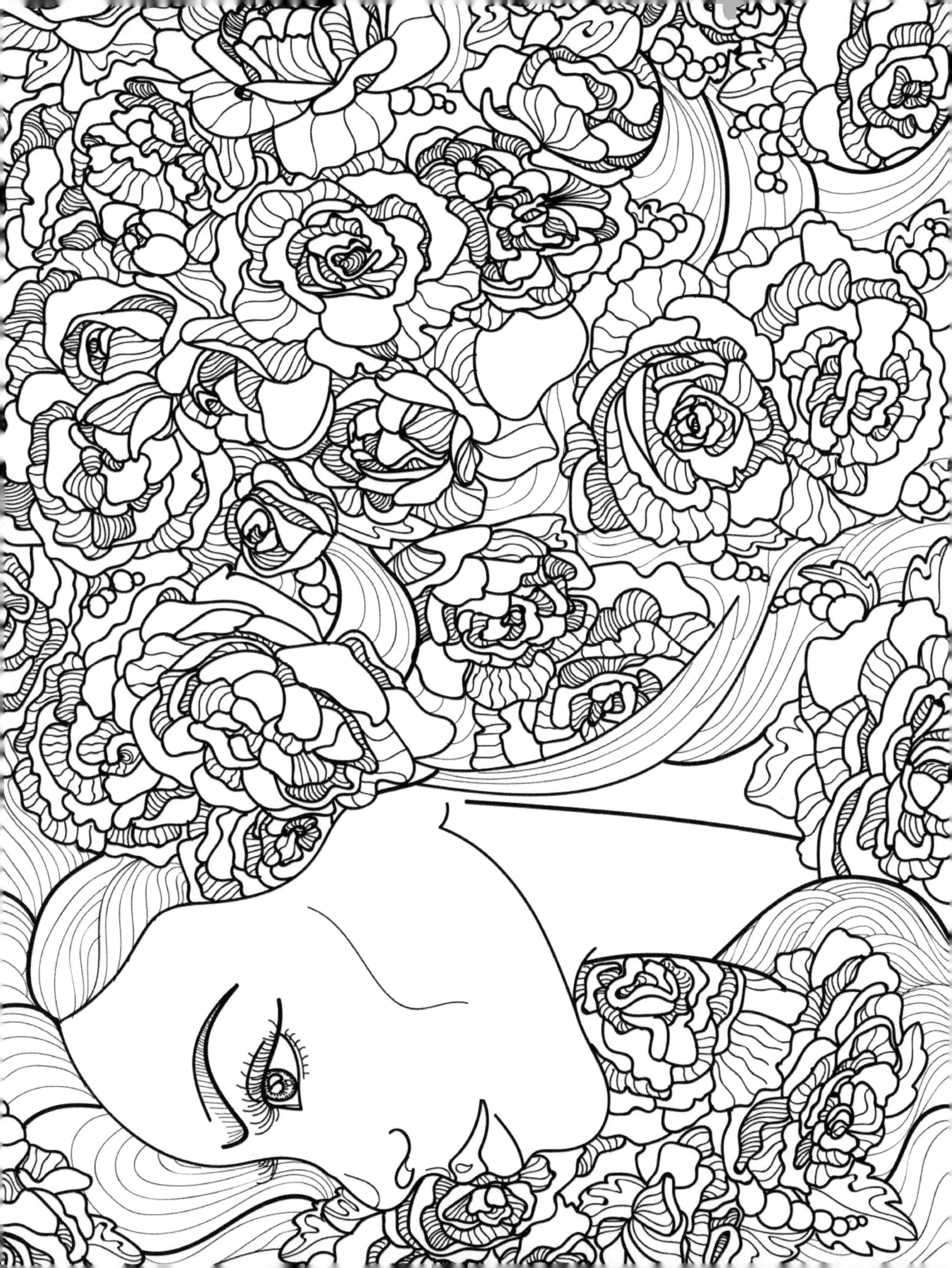

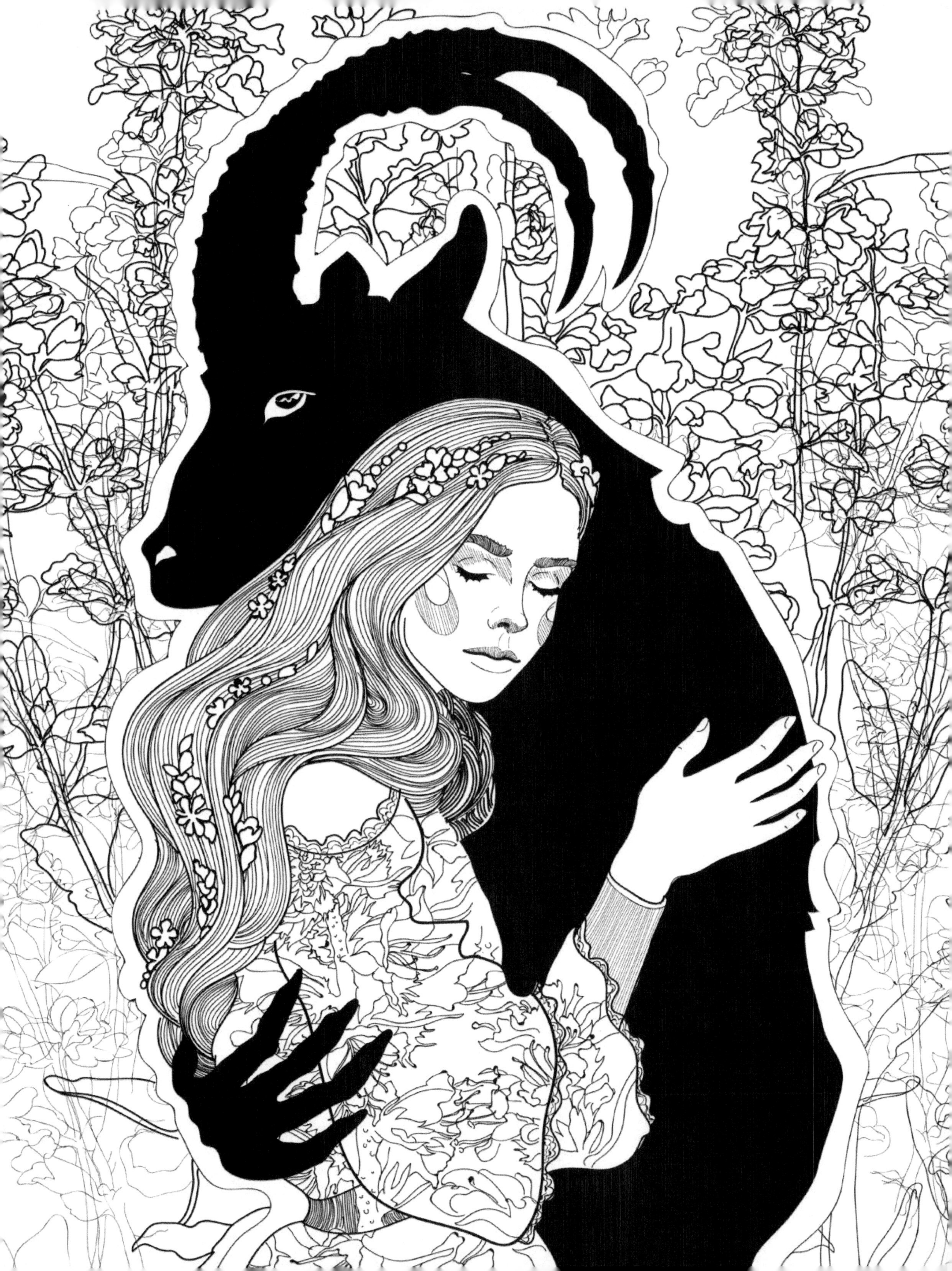

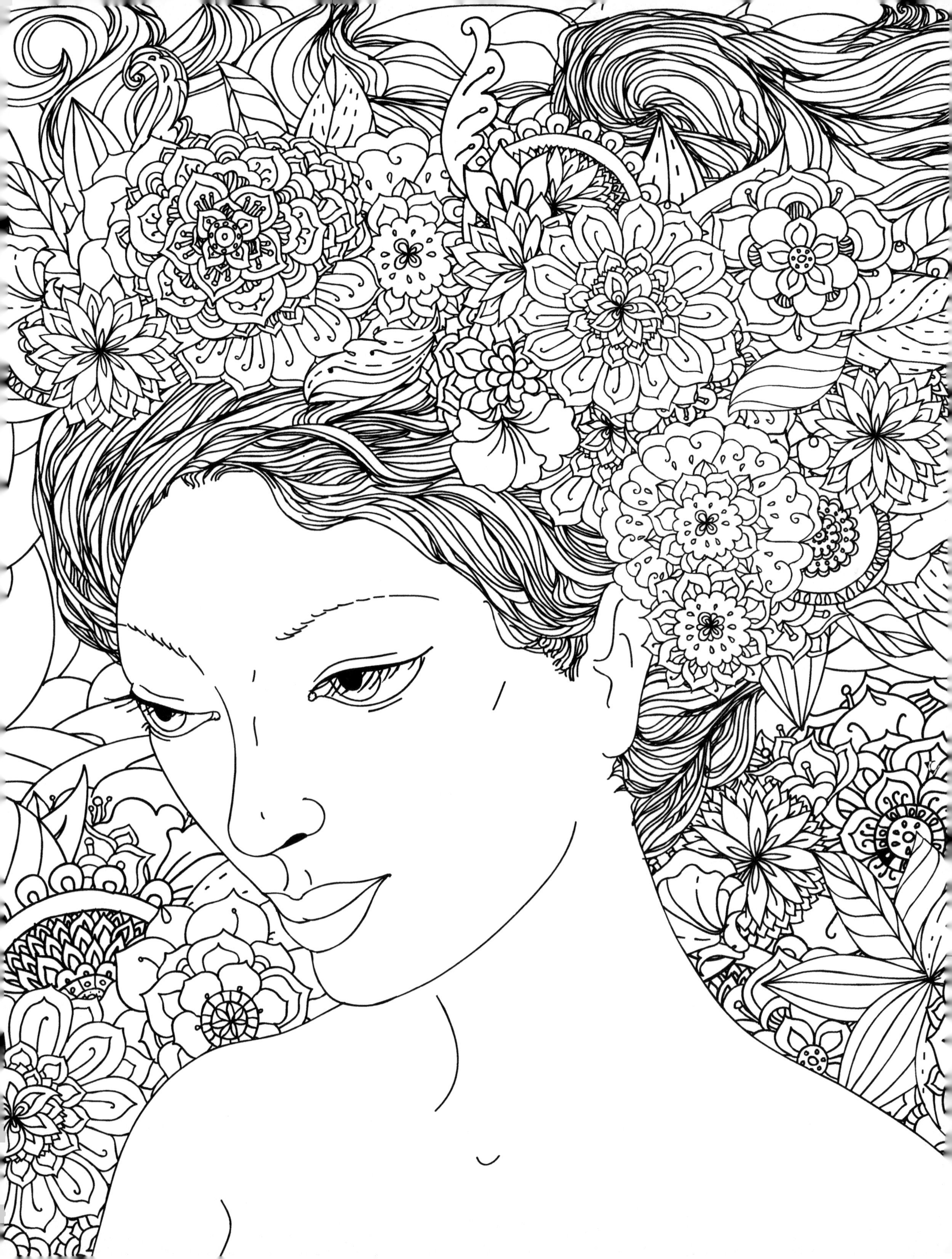

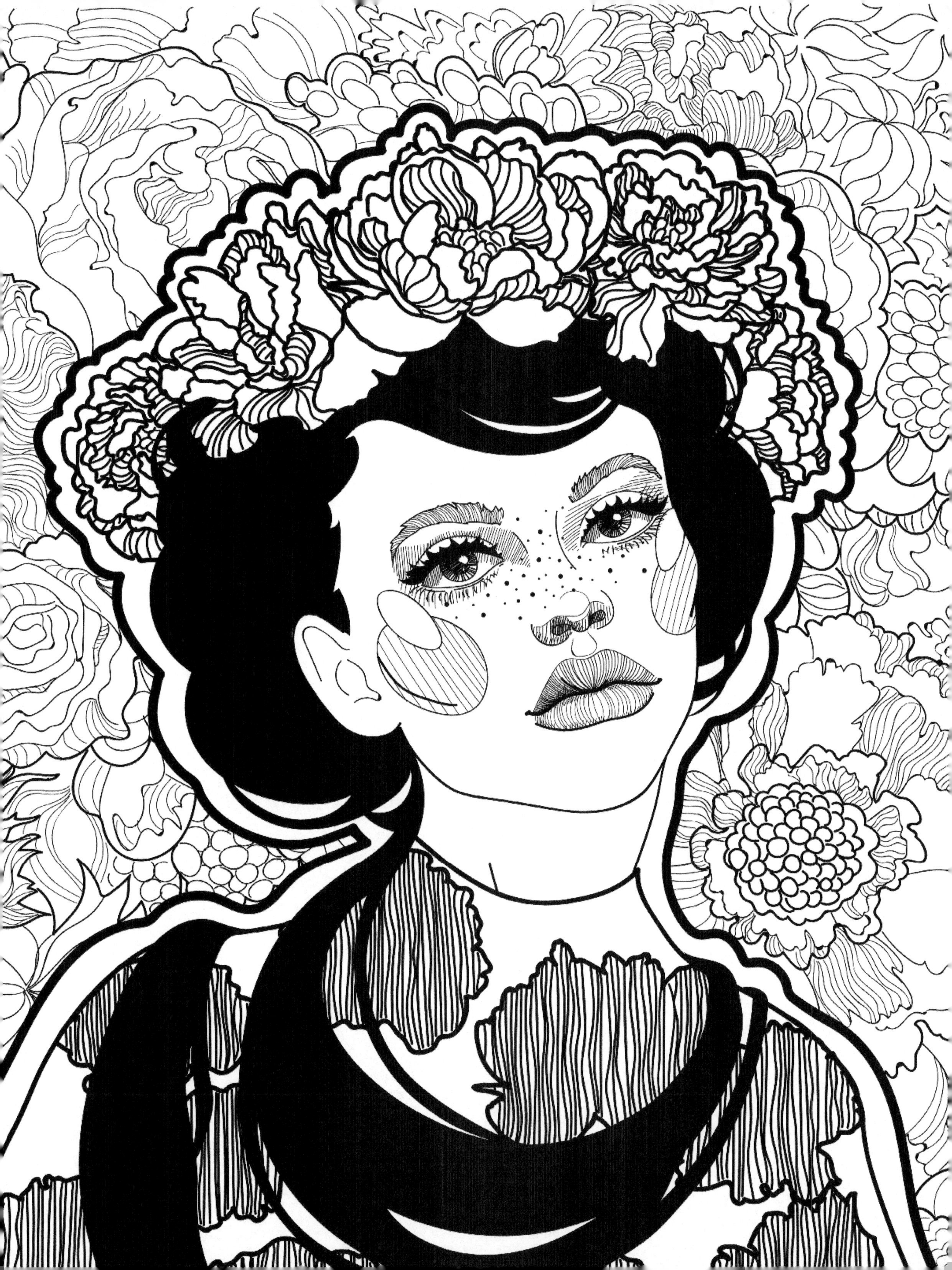

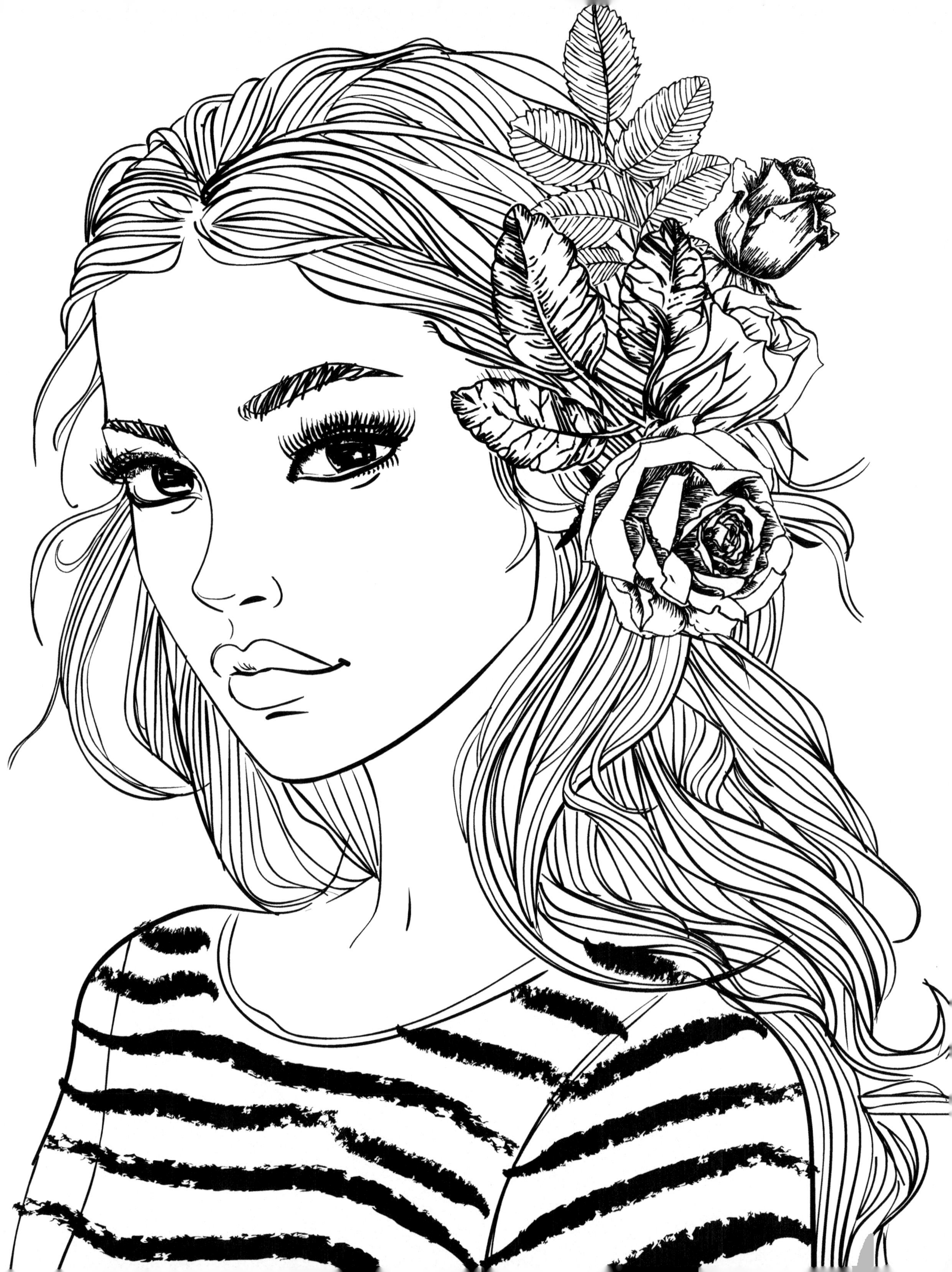

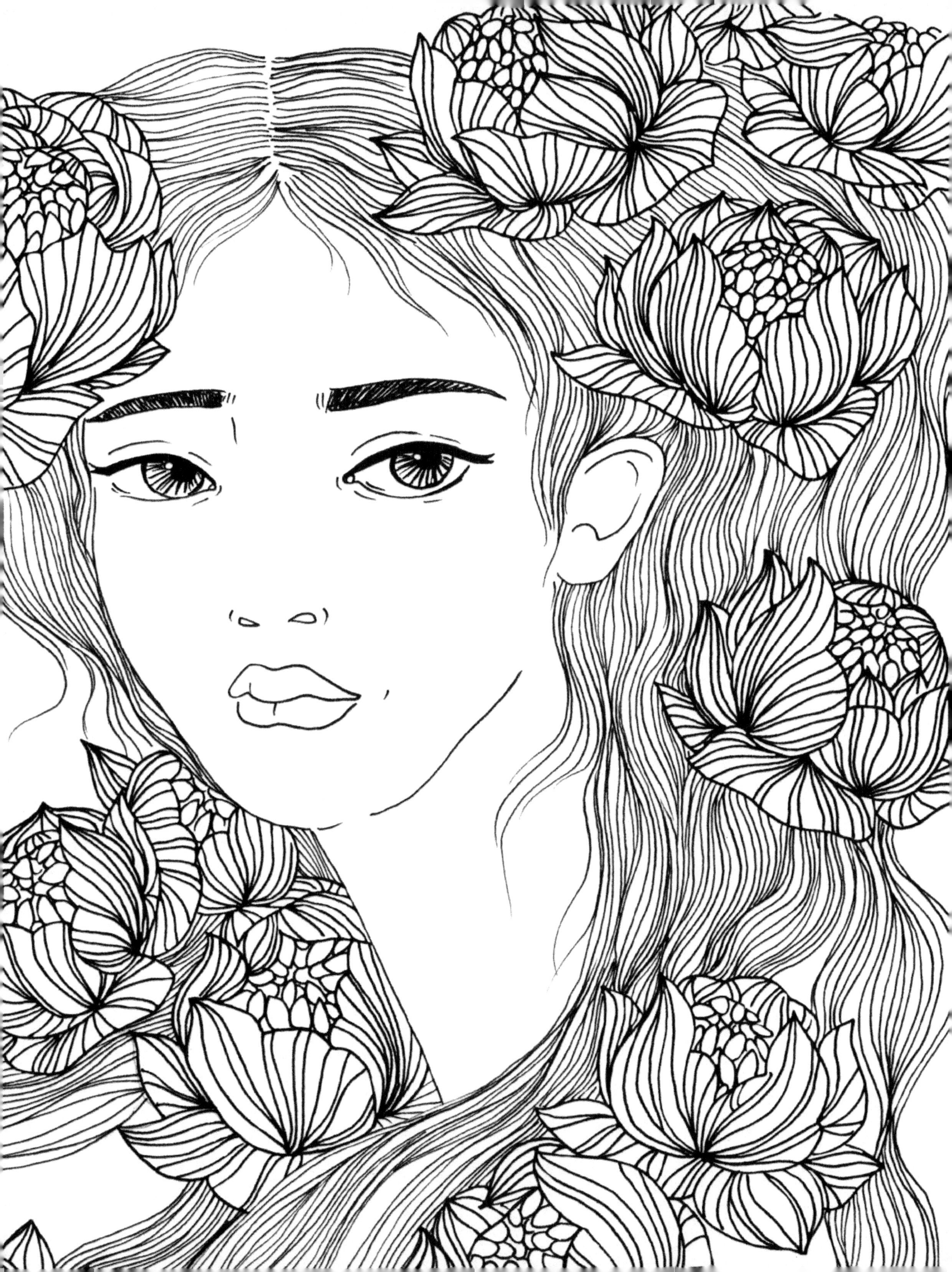

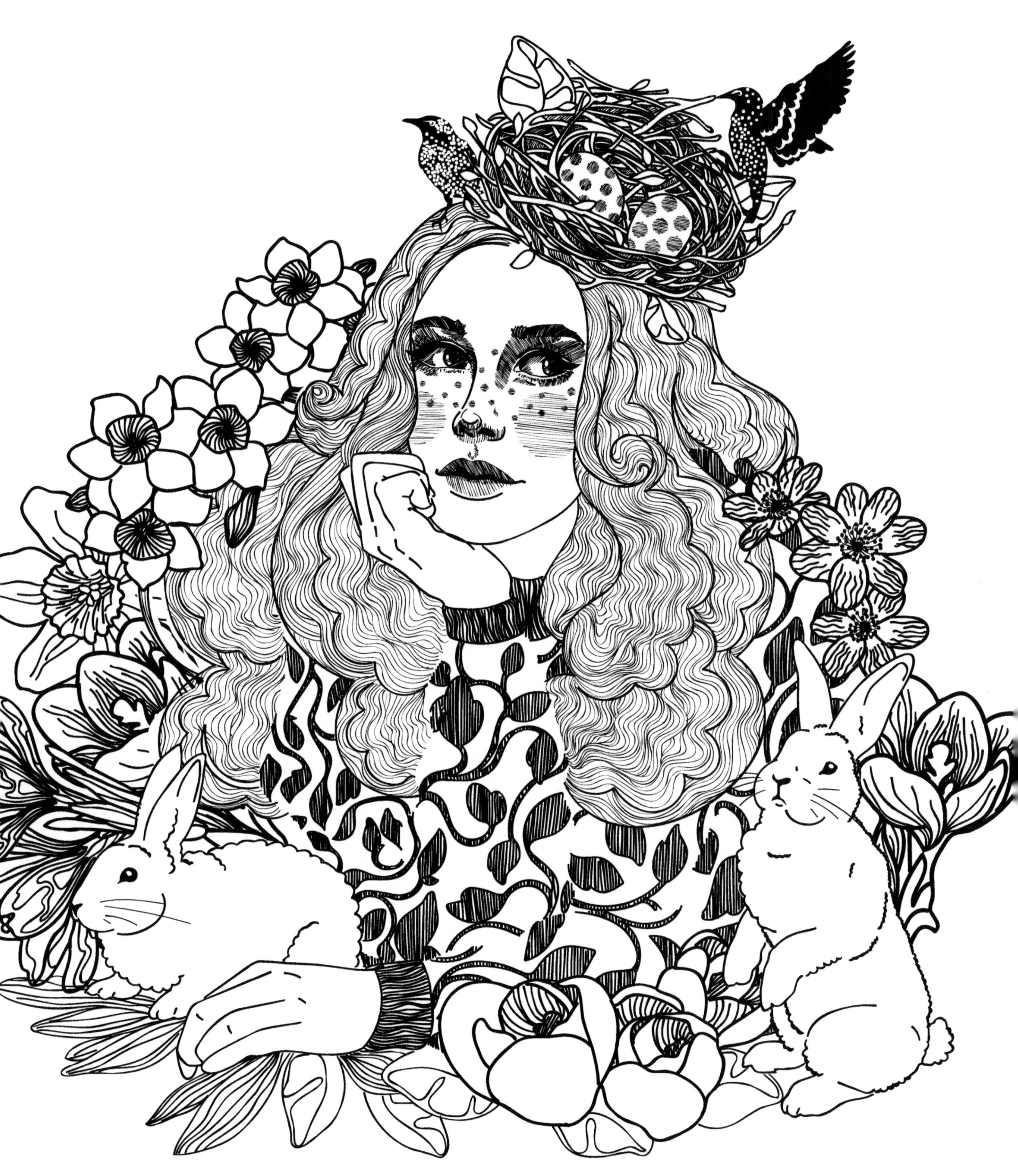

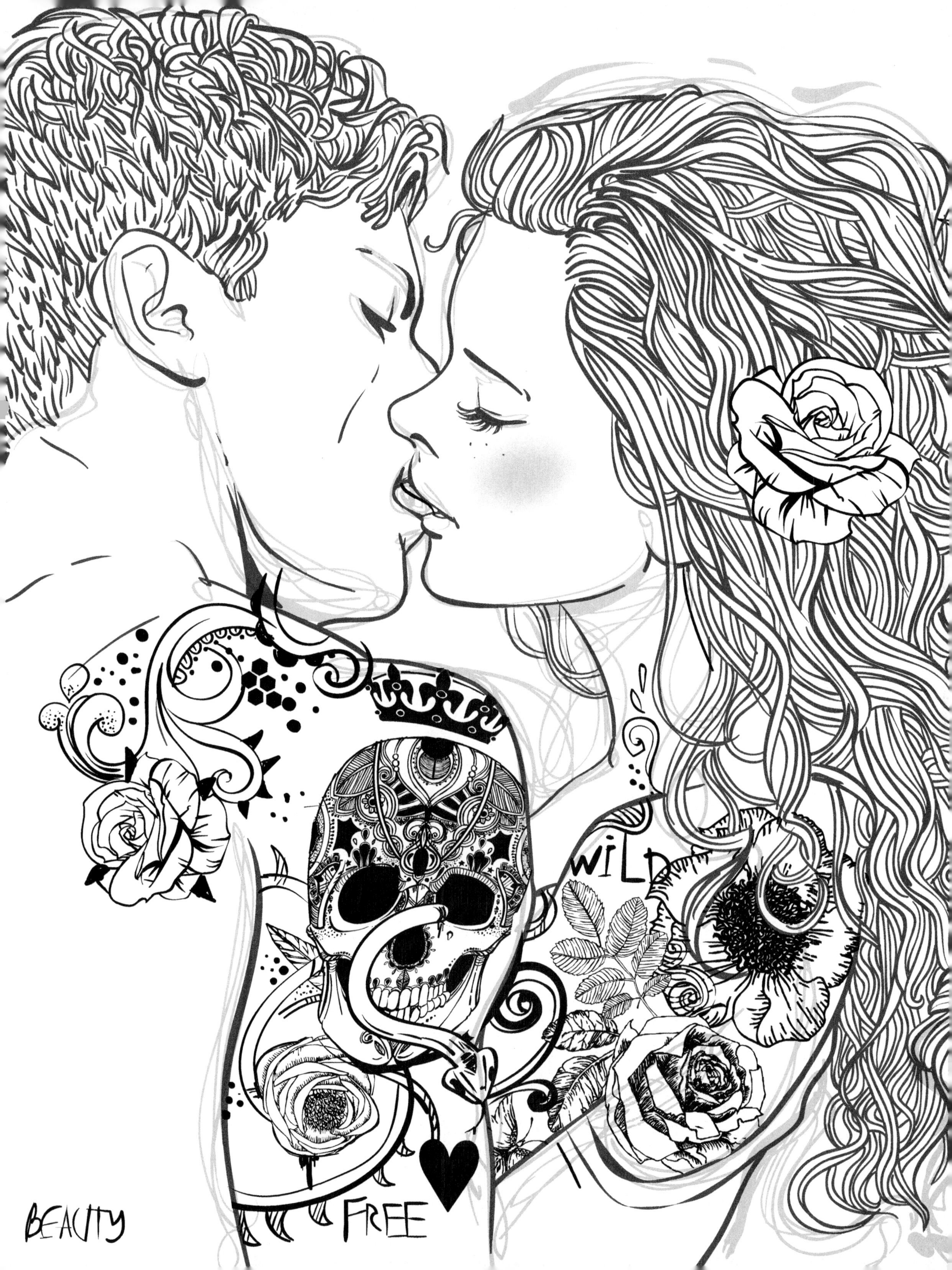

BEAUTY
FREE
WILD

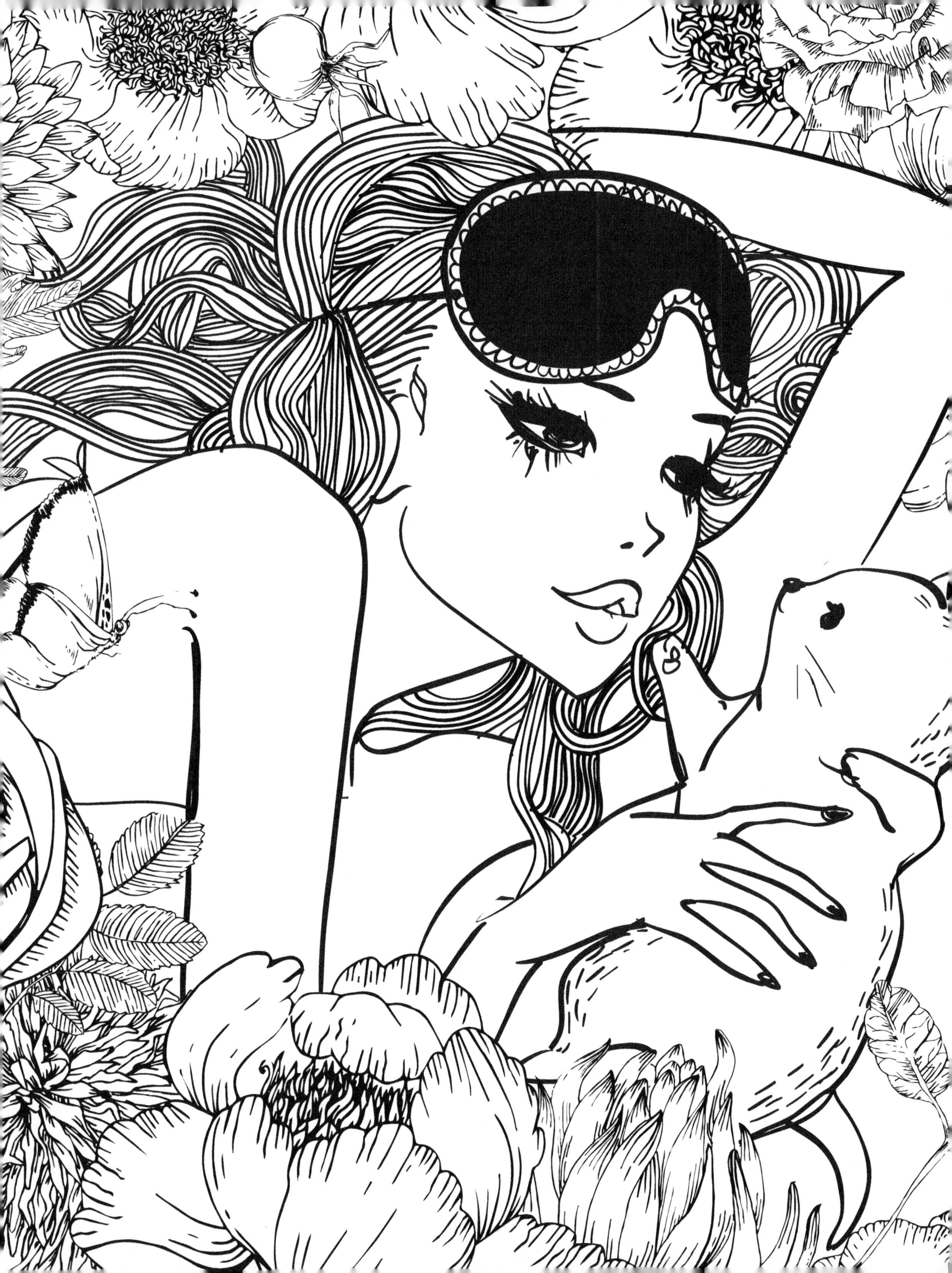

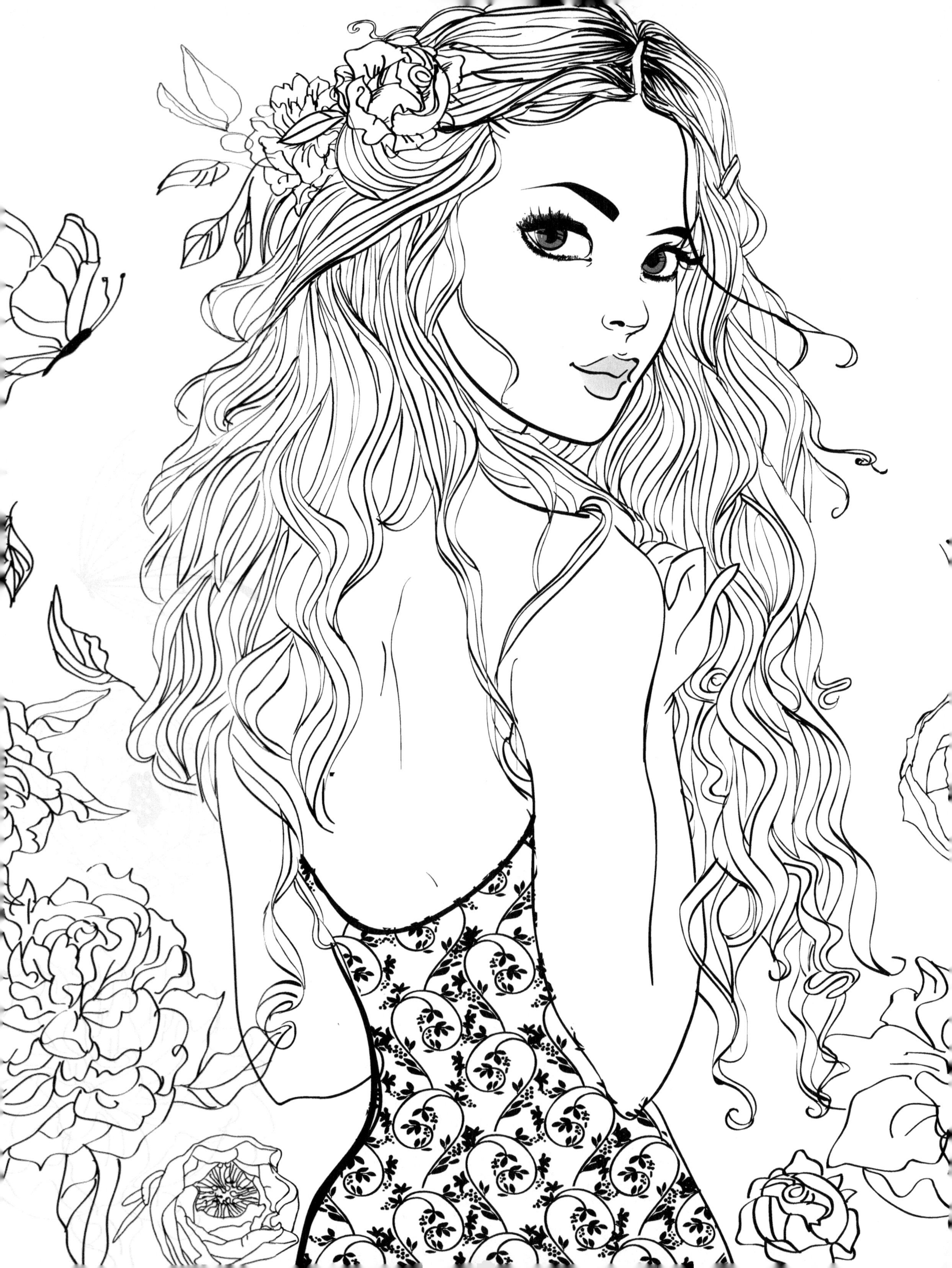

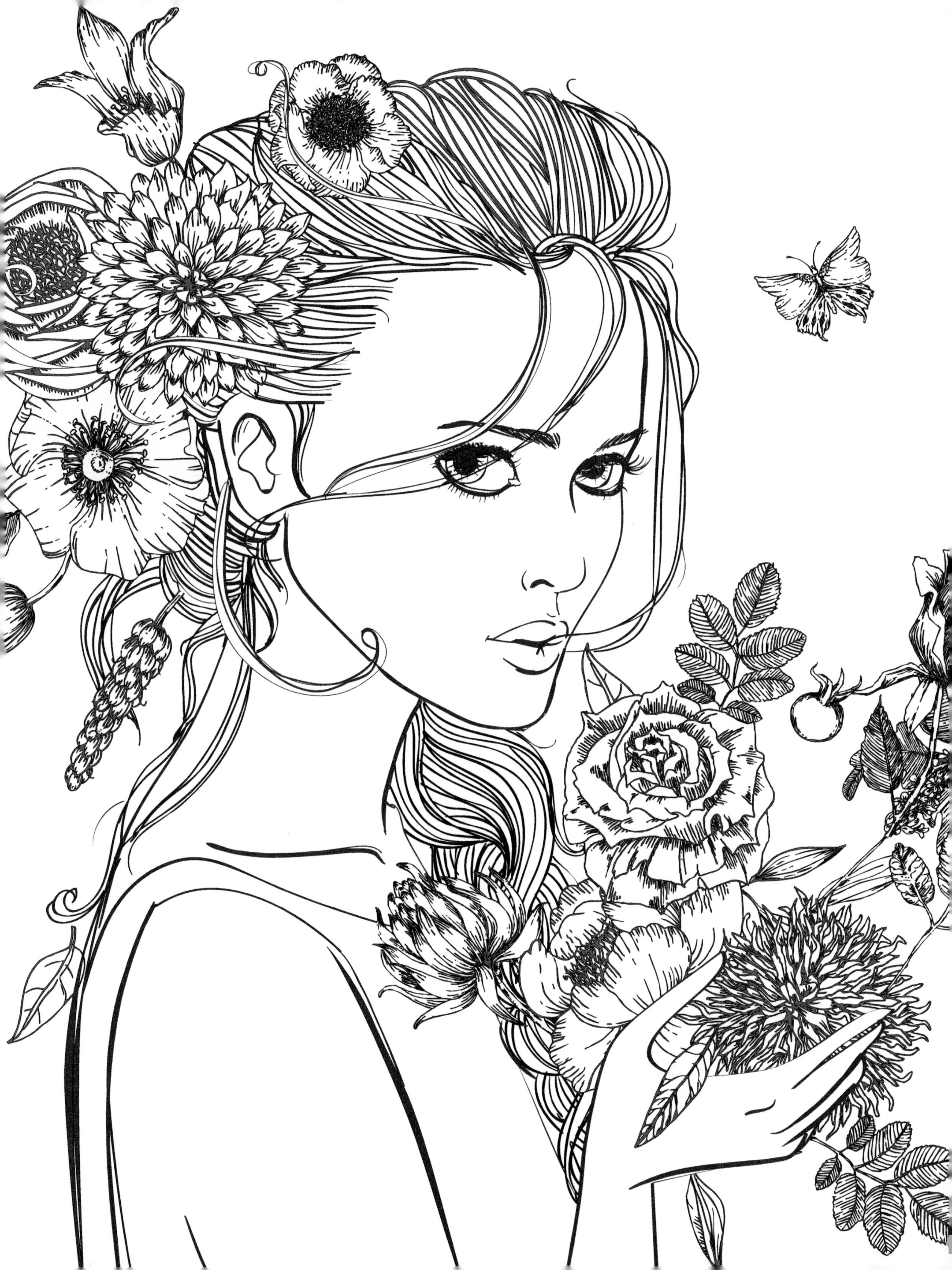

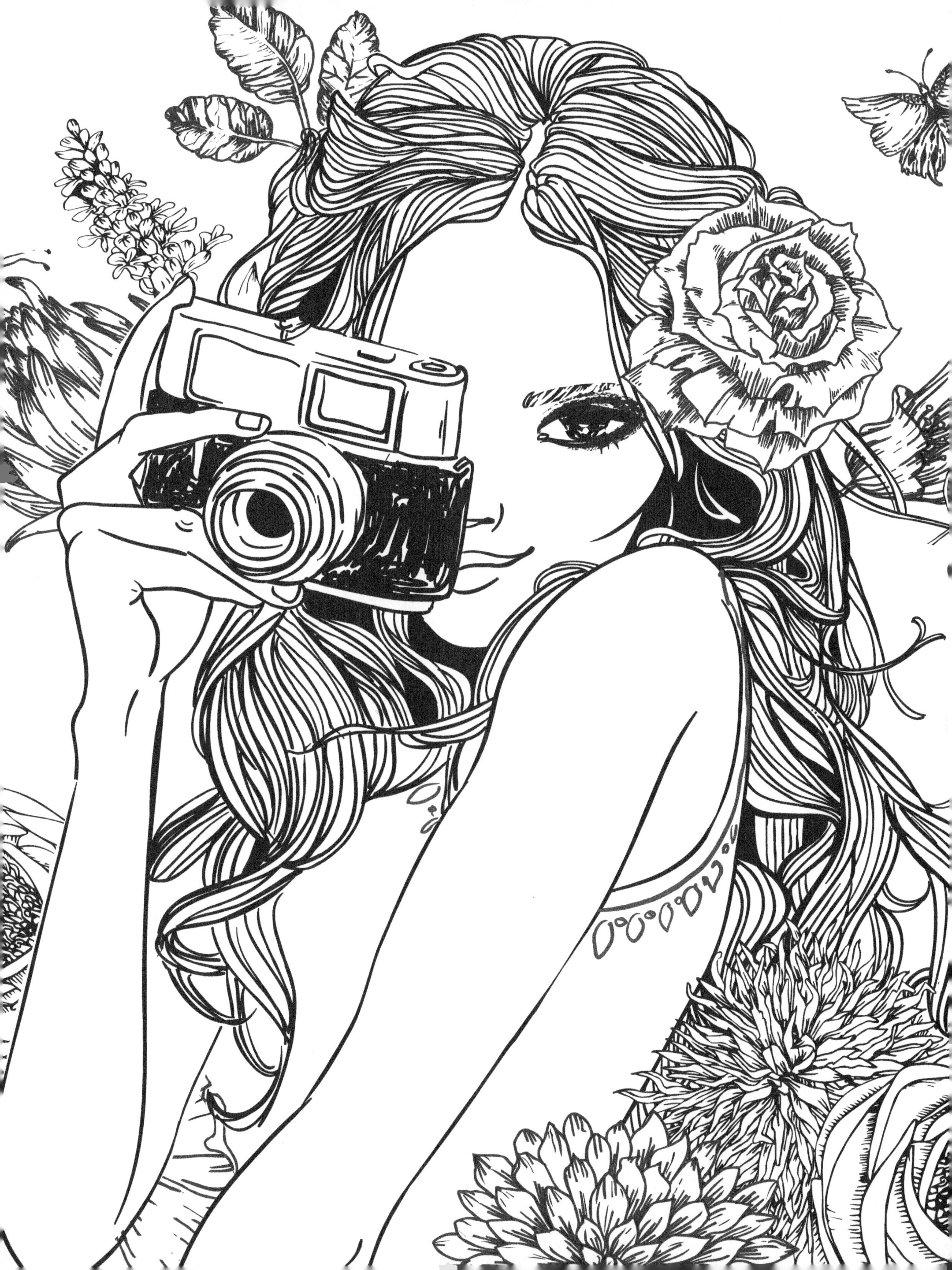

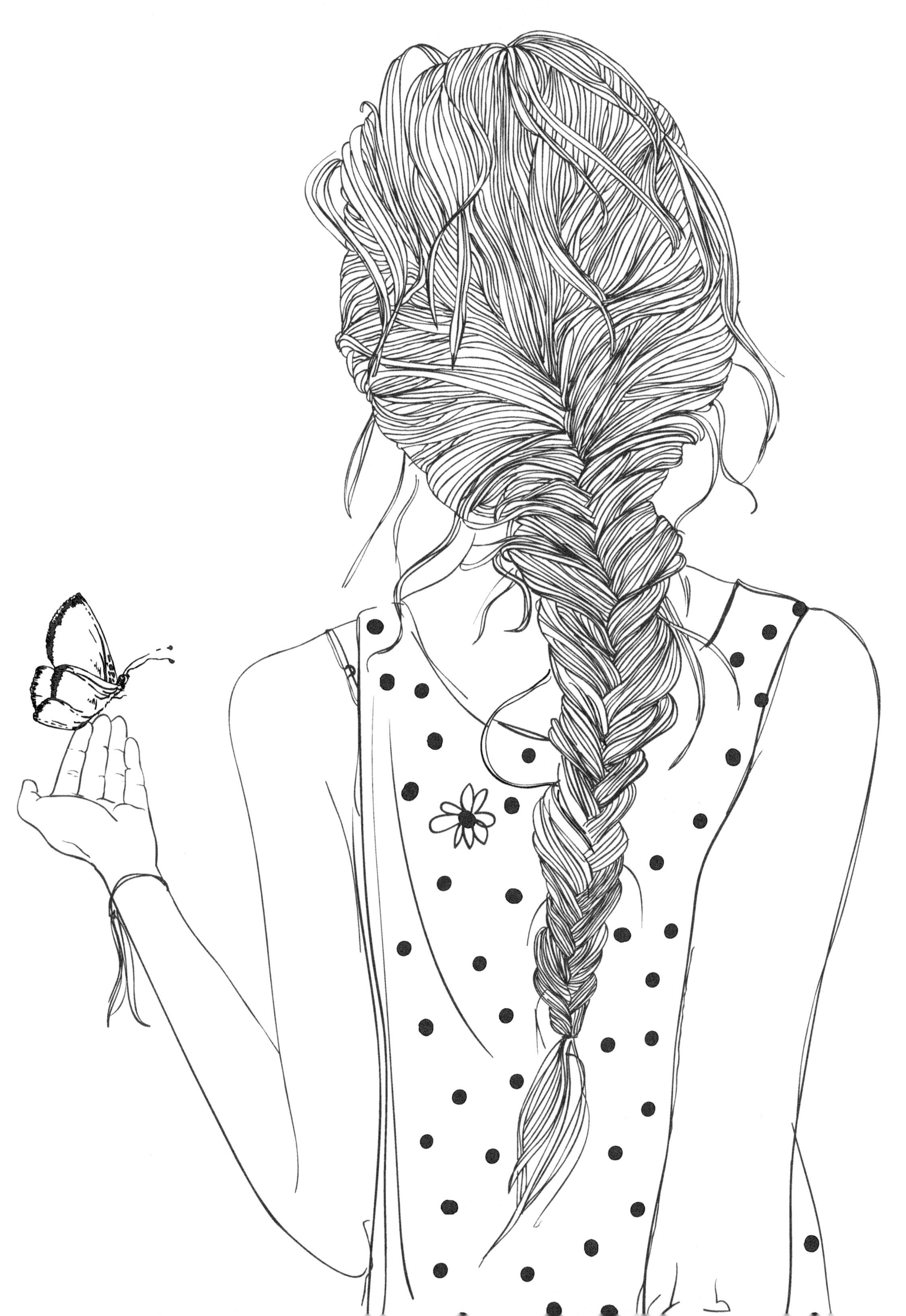

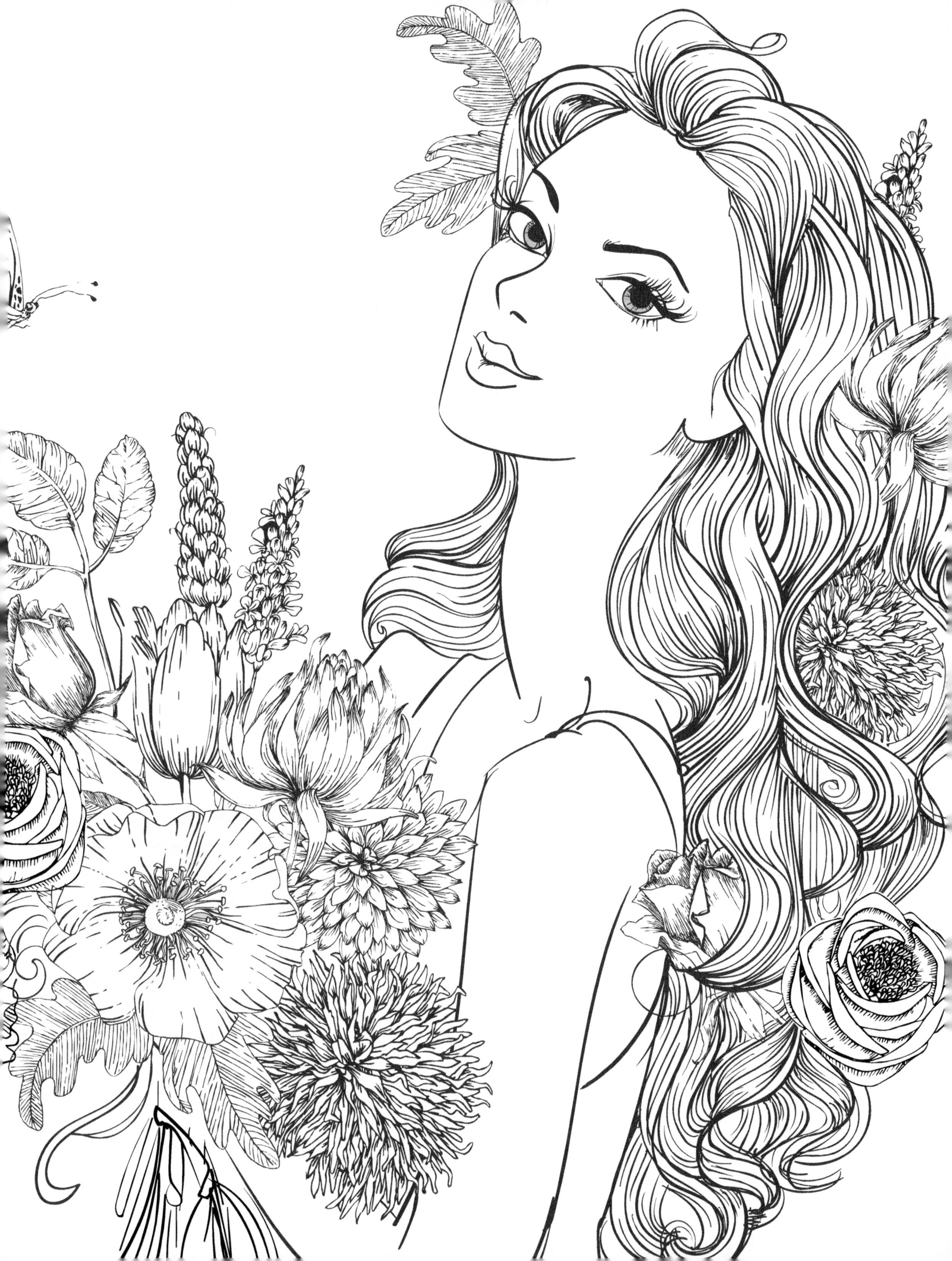

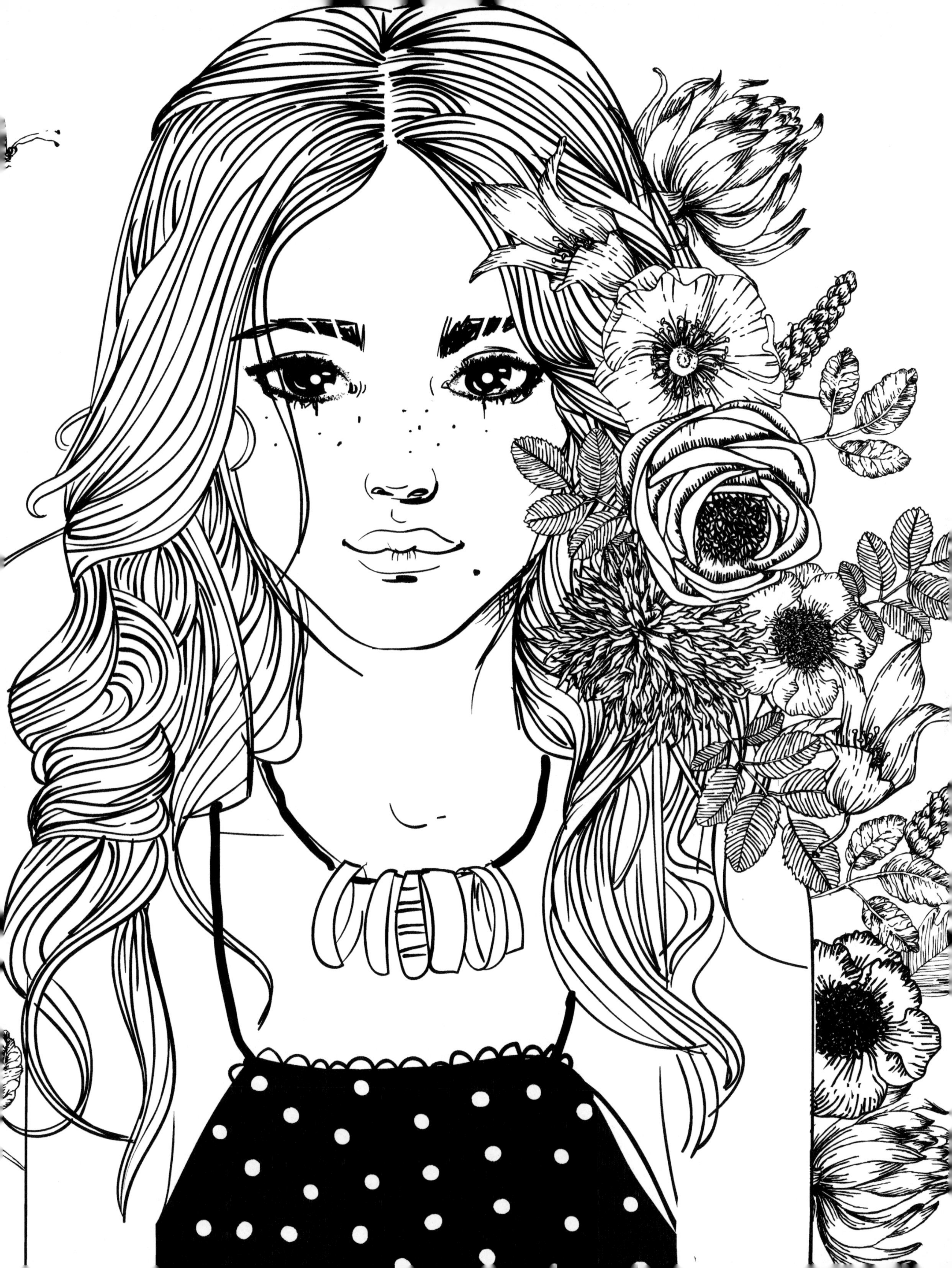

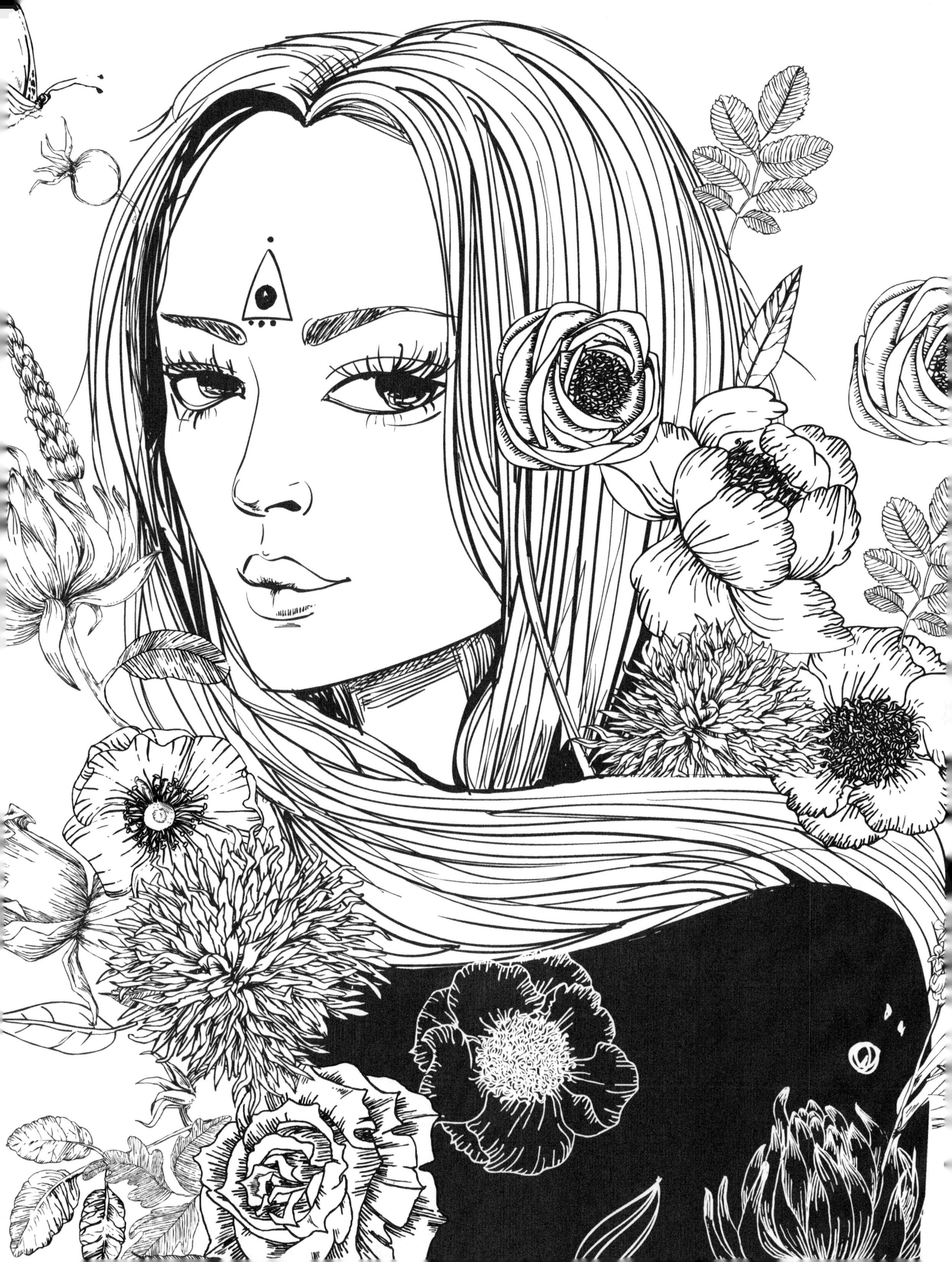

Printed in Great Britain
by Amazon

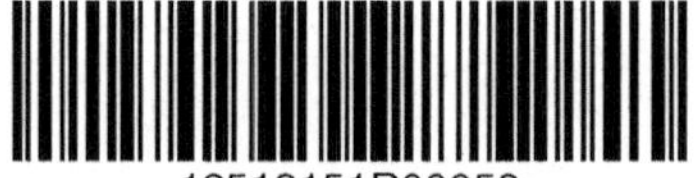
12518151R00059